Wash
Your Brain

Stories. Laughter.
Yoga. Life.

Donna Debs

Illustrations by Mike Goldstein

Wash Your Brain: Stories. Laughter. Yoga. Life.
Published by WanderWonder Books
Wayne, PA

ISBN: 978-1-7374221-1-2
HUMOR / Essays

Cover and interior design by Victoria Wolf,
wolfdesignandmarketing.com, copyright owned by
Donna Debs

Illustrations by Mike Goldstein

For Ray,
the best decision I ever made

Contents

Before You Read:
Scrub

One day, while hanging upside down in a headstand in my yoga studio, tethered by ropes bolted to a thick, sturdy wall so I wouldn't land on the floor but hover above it, I tried to get clear about the name of the column I was about to write for newspapers in the Philadelphia area, much as you would play with the name of a new dog.

I was working out the answer while not thinking about it at all.

That's the way it is with headstand, or *sirsasana* in Sanskrit. It's the king of all yoga poses because of what it does to your mind. Think of the mind as a tornado stuck inside a car wash stuck inside a tall Mardi Gras hurricane drink in New Orleans before you learn how to manage your liquor. Every day, that poor trapped brain is being attacked from all directions, all corners, all people and things and events and worst of all, those crazy self-delusional thoughts swirling around your own chaotic noodle.

When I go upside down in headstand, either straight on the crown of my head or hanging from a set of ropes—my favorite way when I want to stay a long time in the hopes of returning to sanity—my brain gets cleansed. What I thought I couldn't fathom or tackle or laugh about ten minutes before gets scrubbed, and here I am with a new idea—possibly brilliant?—on how to carry on.

In fact, that's the way the great yogi B. K. S. Iyengar apparently said it when discussing how to start fresh, how to make progress when you're stuck: wash your brain.

That's how I came up with the name of my column—"Upside Down"—and the name of this book—*Wash Your Brain*—by hanging upside down and realizing these stories are about getting a cleaner perspective on things that make me feel curious, contemplative, crazy, embarrassed, dumb. In fact, that's why I started writing the column in the first place: to wash my brain and get a handle on what I couldn't handle, mostly by laughing at it. I wanted to find a way around issues that would make my mind dart like a drone, even if as a yogi I was standing right side up, appearing to be firm on the ground like a strong, solid mountain—*tadasana*—another quintessential yoga pose.

As a longtime writer and a longtime yoga teacher, I've always worked to make time for these two disciplines yet not mix them up. They were separate parts, like the mafia guy who loves his family but makes a living as a hit man. I thought my yoga students wouldn't get that other side of me— baffled, bungling, boisterous. At the same time, I thought my column readers would get confused, too, see me as preachy, out there.

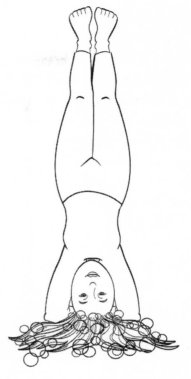

Hey, I've been confused myself.

As time has gone on, though, I've brought these two ends closer, because as much as I'd like to simultaneously live by the Mediterranean Sea *and* by my family on the East Coast of America, I can't. Like a headstand or a mountain pose, I need to find the midline of balance.

Besides, as I've collected stories for this book, I've recognized while standing on my feet or my head that it's all one thing. The stuff I write about defuses that tornado tension so I can teach, and the stuff I learn from teaching shows me how to spend more time as the quiet mountain, so my writing becomes clearer. It's a two-way cleanse!

Still, I know the tornado only too well.

I've started from that point in this book, and as you read on, I hope the decades I've spent in the yoga studio have allowed me to gradually land these tales on the brighter, lighter side of things, to go upside down so I can stand right side up, learning to see with a newly washed brain.

I hope your brain gets a good washing, too.

Layer One:
Blundering

Because I'm a yoga teacher in addition to a writer, people expect I know where to put my arms and legs, which I've proven too often is pathetically untrue. People also expect I can touch my toes without a pole—which fortunately is true, hallelujah—though many of them can't. They tell me this on a regular basis. They also say they don't have enough stability to do yoga, can't bend and flex, can't twist and turn. Or they can't sit quietly, can't concentrate, can't meditate, can't stop the thoughts, the feelings, the impulse to get up and run. Or truthfully, they hate the whole idea and, by the way, they couldn't care less.

That last one I accept completely—to each their own form of pain and redemption. But to the rest, my response is always the same: "Why do you think I do it?"

My mom used to say I was a bull in a china shop—mindless, flailing, dangerous. My sister Caryl claims I've always been graceful, but I think she tries to make me feel better for having broken a couple of bones. Okay, seven.

My sister Shara laughs when I dance, and I don't think it's with me but at me. And my husband, Ray, says nothing on the subject of my natural poise. He doesn't want to jinx the lull in unplanned events that end in a hospital or on the floor of a fancy restaurant.

Fortunately, the answer to bashing and crashing can often be found in the yoga studio. If I can turn myself upside down into restorative *viparita karani*, a simple legs-up-the-wall pose with the back flat on the ground—even with a cast on a leg—I can find a clean perspective, and a new story, on my latest relapse. I stand redeemed, even if I can't stand without a pair of crutches.

Alert the emergency room, I'm using the snowblower

A gainst my better judgment, one day I learned how to use the snowblower we finally bought after years of either shoveling by hand or paying some embarrassing fee for a guy with a big shovel attached to a macho truck to come to our rescue and make Ray look like a puny weightlifting failure.

"My savior," I would croon as the BTOD, Big Truck on Driveway, lifted the barrier between us and the outside world as easily as Superman lifted his damsel, Lois Lane.

Not anymore.

"You're not gonna believe how easy this is," said Ray, as he rolled the new orange robot out of the garage after a big snowfall. And then with the patience usually reserved for people paying him money, he proceeded to give me enough directions to make me look longingly at our silent shovels hanging frozen in time, relics once worthy of custom-created hooks on the dingy garage wall.

The lesson formally began with him saying the snow-blower weighed two hundred pounds, almost twice my size, and ended with a deep pause, a penetrating stare, and an emphatic warning that, should I ever find the whirling dervish getting further and further away from the house with me being dragged along like a mound of slush, I should "JUST LET GO AND IT WILL STOP."

In between the rollout and the fear of doom, he said something about a choke which sounded like the most counter-intuitive mechanical process ever created. He said, "Put the lever in the open position for off and the closed position for on." Because I looked like he was speaking an Inuit tongue, he leapt over the machine and grabbed my throat for show.

"See, I'm choking you and the choke is on, but your throat is cut off."

Since I lacked enough blood to nod, he kept modeling the action until his handprints became stained on my neck like sunburn on an ice cube. Then we both started gasping because he'd forgotten to turn the real choke on, or maybe off, and we were inhaling giant balls of smoky fumes.

"JUST LET GO AND MAKE IT STOP," I sputtered, and he swaggered back to the machine like a cowboy to his horse and finally choked—or unchoked—it instead of me.

It was the look on Ray's face when I took our new family member out for an inaugural stroll, giving it an encouraging pat on its square bottom, that made me start swaggering myself in defiance because his head was cocked sideways, and he was staring bemused like I was a kid learning to ride a bike. He was curious to see if I could keep the thing moving safely straight ahead, or if I'd lose a toe to the churning shark teeth spitting out pure white and hopefully nothing red or flesh-toned.

He has seen me burned, stabbed, sprained, and broken by everyday events so often that he waited with a mixture of entertainment and fear, wondering if this would be my finest hour or my latest trip to the emergency room.

He also knows I need to understand how everything works down to the smallest minutiae, and when a giant *Aha!* goes off that rivals the big bang, I begin babbling about why I didn't become a world-class scientist and perhaps there is still time to rethink my career.

Except by the next day when he suggested I practice my skills, the idea seemed as foreign to me as if we were on the ocean and the driveway was underwater. I couldn't even remember how to get the machine out of the garage. Do I have to turn it on first? What if it rams into my car? What if I forget to open the garage door and my snowblower and I die from our respective chokes?

I even mashed and bloodied a finger pressing my password into the garage keypad. Pressing is not as harmless as it seems if you approach the task hoping your finger will prevent you from proceeding any further.

So what do I do when the big snow comes? Do I nostalgically reach for the shovel, backbreaking or not, or should

I be brave and conquer the orange churner though the thought makes my hands and feet curl tightly to my body?

Or should I climb to the top of the roof—wearing a wind-blown dress, high heels, and red lipstick of course—and pray that Superman, with his X-ray vision and Big Truck, is just about ready to round the corner?

Feasting on the medical buffet

Asthma, boils, chickenpox, dog bites, eczema, fractures. There's something for every letter of the alphabet out there.

The world is a smorgasbord of accidents and ills, bizarre things like the elephantiasis and two-headedness I ogled as a kid in books of medical oddities. Yet I didn't anticipate I'd eventually be sampling every one of them, perhaps deciding which I'd choose for my final reckoning.

Never though, until I became a cautious adult, did I ever have a bug sleeping in my ear.

I'd been fearing this for decades. Ever since a friend, an emergency room doc, shared everyone's worst nightmare: a cockroach inside the auditory receptacle of a screaming patient stricken in the middle of the night between dreams of green pastures and nightmares of medieval torture.

As the on-call resident he had to root out the victim's sudden sense of acute itchiness—he had to explore, he had to probe. Using his best resources, nausea aside, he had to get the damn crawly thing out.

He never told me exactly how he did it, which could have prevented me from collecting dangerous implements to stage an attack. I stopped just short of a kitchen knife, because believe me, the thought of a bug in the body can make a person want to cut their heart out. I once had a mosquito fly inside my plaster leg cast, unremovable, so I speak from the insane asylum.

At first, in this new predawn adventure, I thought I was having an allergy attack or a reaction to a hair product or maybe it was that trek in the woods where I brushed up against a critter. I once had sixteen chigger bites on my buttock from a nap on the grass gone awry, so I'm no virgin. I know bugs love intimate inter-species encounters.

"Get out of bed!" I screamed to Ray. "Something is alive in my ear!"

"It's just you being you," he muttered. "You know how you are."

Yes, I know how I am, a gobbler of the medical smorgasbord. I used to crave pictures of giant growths sticking out of people's necks or bizarre boils bursting and blanketing their hosts, and as a kid I was fascinated with the lifestyle of lepers.

Then I grew up and learned that in health matters, common—not exotic—is definitely the way to go.

"Find me a flashlight!" I yelled. "You gotta look deep."
And he did.

"There's nothing in there," he insisted, piercing my ear canal with the high beam. "In a few hours it'll be gone like last week's wart."

Then he hugged me for a little support, and the itching and kicking went ballistic from the inside out.

We ran to the bathroom, and he agitated me half upside down, half sideways. Clearly, something was stuck in me like damp salt in a shaker.

If my doctor friend had told me years ago the way to get rid of a bug in the ear is to pour warm oil into the canal—mineral, olive, WD-40, who cares?—I would have had a plan. He didn't, and I can assure you in the middle of such an event you do not stop to Google.

Fortunately, for all of us, this inner-cochlear connection with another breed doesn't happen much, unless—if you're daffy—you sweeten the odds with bright light and honey. Yet even without that, bugs sometimes like the small, cozy space of an available slot, much like we adore squeezing into the middle seat in the last row of a crowded airplane.

We love that, right?

So, in the darkness of the witching hour on a freaky Friday in September 2017—with no plan—Ray and I shook harder and harder, and a long, slippery, black thing slid out of my ear and landed on the bathroom floor. It wasn't doing any better than me. It wasn't a cockroach, a small miracle in itself; maybe it was a weevil.

And though I swear I never kill a bug no matter where I find it, I put this struggling fellow or girl out of its misery. Perhaps it, too, was sampling the vast array of possibilities, trying out options for its own final day of reckoning.

The bug certainly found its answer, but for me, I'm happy to live another day and take my chances on the next item to be offered along the tasty and abundant medical buffet.

Margaritas can
be *mucho loco*

A single sip of a "Bahama Mama" once landed me on the floor with four Caribbean bartenders staring down, the latest tourist casualty crumpled like a corn chip.

Right then, with the moon over the horizon and my ego at the bottom of the sea, I swore off any alcoholic drink that's pink or blue—maybe a dastardly combination of liquors, juices, sugars, sunscreen, sea glass, conch shells. Who knows what they put in there?

No pink or blue for me, I vowed. One evening of sheer humiliation decades ago was enough. Caribbean concoctions are not for me. Period.

Yet I must confess a continuing fascination with one festive Mexican potion in a tall, wide glass with salt on its rim and a fresh slice of lime perched on its icy top. Thanks to Mother Nature, tequila is white or gold, and limes are green. No conflict there.

I love margaritas—the taste, the chunky glasses, the crunchy chips and salsa on the side, the guacamole made from another green thing called "fruit of the gods." Who can argue with God?

A margarita is a fiesta, a vacation, livin' *la vida loca*.

Problem is, I'm still the ultimate lightweight. One of these drinks has enough sugar and alcohol to send me back to the Bahamas in a box. But thanks to the sheer force of marketing, there's an answer, the so-called Skinnygirl Margarita.

Fewer calories, less sugar, stylish bottle, trendy ponytailed woman on the label who I will no doubt become if I buy the product.

Skinnygirl first arrived on my doorstep in the hands of my equally sensitive sister, Shara. It felt like the latest consumer breakthrough, like the Post-it Note or the rolling suitcase. Why didn't we think of it? Since the margarita was invented in the 1930s, could this be the first time it was bottled for sissy women like us?

Yet the margarita has a celebrated history. It was apparently created for a socialite, or a showgirl, or someone's daughter—all named some version of Marjorie, Marguerite, or Margarita. Or some say it was concocted for Rita Hayworth. Really?

It seems Rita was born Margarita, and legend says some guy who loved her named it when she was a dancer in, get this, Tijuana. *La vida loca,* Rita!

Rita may have loved her drink, but this bottled brand tastes as flat as Rita was not. The idea, however, rocks. Thus, with my baby sister in tow, the quest began for the perfect, to-die-for "skinny."

Since neither of us can handle more than one, the quest was about prolonging the experience while driving every bartender between here and the Yucatan *mucho loco*. Premium tequila, less tequila, no Triple Sec, no Grand Marnier, no sweet-and-sour mix, no sugar, no agave syrup, more lime, itty bitty bit of salt. We were in constant search of "the one" that basically had no margarita ingredients at all yet would give us a rollicking good time while sucking on the ice at the end of the glass.

Sometimes we even shared one. Now that's really skinny!

Out on the town one night, and doing a little private research on the subject, I ran into a bravado bartender determined to prove his kosher salt. Instead of sweet-and-sour mix, he used orange juice. Instead of Grand Marnier or Triple Sec for sweetness, he used Sweet'N Low. Sweet'N Low? Why didn't we think of that?

The drink looked orange, but not being pink or blue, my vow was intact. I lifted the straw, took one sip, and as the liquid went from my head to my stomach and back again, I imagined Rita Hayworth, J. Lo, Penélope Cruz, and all those other lovely Latinas staring down praying I wasn't going to embarrass them as the words "tourist casualty" floated above.

What happened? Let's just say Margaritaville may be a state of mind in certain hot, steamy countries, but to some of us, it's a state of no return. Fortunately, I was able to lie down for a tiny unobtrusive rest before the bartender had to carry me out.

After I was swept off the floor, and the fog cleared, I realized my mistake. The Sweet'N Low wrapper ... *it's pink!* And the official tequila plant ... *it's the blue agave!* Pink and blue, again. Oh, *Dios mio!*

Yard cleanup in 74 easy steps

Fast as the ants return to the kitchen in spring, you can make a clean sweep of yard work with a hop, skip, and jump around your little patch of earth. Try these quick and easy stress-free steps:

1. Grab pointy sticks in two bunches
2. Wash and sterilize bloody cuts
3. Find garden glove for one hand
4. Find ski glove for other
5. Regather dumb pointy sticks
6. Search for eco-friendly trash bags
7. Wish you had eco-friendly trash bags
8. Scratch itchy nose because of allergies
9. Clean mud off nose
10. Break sticks in half so they fit in tiny bag
11. Ponder if they're twigs, sticks, branches, or limbs
12. Meditate
13. Pick up big mother branch
14. Place ice near right eye

15. Realize sun is blinding you for first time in months
16. Search for sunglasses
17. Empty two drawers searching
18. Wonder why you haven't seen neighbors all winter
19. See one and chat
20. Remember why you haven't seen neighbors all winter
21. Fall over acorns
22. Wrap ice pack around knee
23. Relocate gloves
24. Continue to search for sunglasses
25. Drag refuse from woods
26. Remember there are ticks back there and go hunt for repellent
27. Make cup of tea while hunting
28. Meditate
29. Notice you got mud on floor
30. Clean floor without taking off boots
31. Start again
32. Track down sunglasses, finally
33. Relocate one glove, search for other one
34. Notice lamppost is leaning though husband said he fixed it
35. Get angry
36. Let off steam by dragging loose boulder
37. Wash and sterilize bloody cuts
38. Rake leaves so you can eat off ground
39. Bend down to try
40. Notice you're wearing pajama bottoms

41. Go in to change
42. Relocate gloves and sunglasses
43. Grab phone because you're expecting call
44. Gather soggy yellow gunk
45. Wonder where you put phone
46. Go inside to look
47. Meditate
48. Gaze at spot that used to feature prized clematis vine
49. Remember you pruned and killed it
50. Punish yourself by dragging dead bush
51. Wash and sterilize bloody cuts
52. Gather sticks that look like wishbones
53. Wish you could find phone
54. Listen to clinking chimes on deck
55. Enter reverie about summer
56. Realize summer comes before fall which comes before winter, again
57. Meditate
58. Pick up pieces of chimney cracked by storms
59. Wash and sterilize bloody cuts
60. Continue to search for phone
61. Prune half-dead tree with rusty garden tool
62. Yank off poor limb
63. Remove ice pack from knee and put on shoulder
64. Trip on broken step
65. Remember insurance company laughed when you asked if they'd fix it
66. Get angry

67. Calm down by sinking hands in dirt
68. Wonder why you're not wearing gloves
69. Wash and sterilize bloody cuts
70. Continue to search for phone
71. Hop, skip, and jump around your little patch of earth
72. Seriously wrench back
73. Lie down
74. Meditate …

What is a complaint, anyway?

With both of us miserable, my old high school buddy, Ellen, and I made a pact. Over a lunch when I had a sprained wrist and she had a sprained arm—our jackets falling off our shoulders, our forks clanging to the floor—we took a no-complaint challenge.

We would not, for one painfully long week, groan about one solitary thing. Not our sore limbs, the rainy weather, our mates, our families, the waitress who won't stop talking, the mediocre veggie burgers, or the devastating state of the world. I mean, the wonderful universe we live in.

Researchers say we generally gripe thirty times a day: "You're late, I'm late, these pants are too tight, this bed is too soft, the kitchen is too messy." We'd be happy, maybe, if only we had a full body massage, a HydraFacial, a houseboy, and a week on an ergonomic beach chair. Some days, with all the drama around us, we complain so much we forget to cook, clean, and work.

Hey, that's not so bad.

But really, what is a complaint?

The first thing Ellen and I did was come up with parameters. For example, is saying "I have nothing to wear" a gripe? Or a fact? For our week of challenge, we called it a fact. Our experiment, our rules.

We realized we needed help. We did a little research and came up with this official definition: Complaining is blaming others or life itself, instead of accepting a situation and trying to make it better.

We screwed up our mouths and pondered. *Hmmm …* tagged, we're it. We took an oath to mend our ways. The week began.

Day One:

Complaining can be good for you. It helps you connect to others and takes a load off the chest, except when a brief cry over *wine* becomes a full-blown bellyache of a *whine* that sends you to the bottom of the bottle. I tried to tease out the differences, and on the first day, aware of my repeated meanders over that fine grumpy line, I turned grumbles into gratitude. Like being thankful I had a TV to watch the news, even if it made me sick. I mean, uh, was thrilled I had eyes to watch.

Day Three:

My friend confessed she was complaining in her heart, though nothing was crossing her lips. She had a neighbor who was driving her crazy. I asked her the latest. I knew if she answered, because of the oath, she'd say she was just glad she had a neighbor. Suddenly, she started laughing because otherwise her throat would explode. Laughing, we say, is better than complaining because people are drawn to happy, optimistic types. If you want to be that sort of person. I mean, who doesn't want to see the glass half full!

Day Five:

We decided complaining may be hard to identify, but everyone knows when "Honey, could you please not put your shoes in the middle of the floor?" becomes "I am sick and tired of you trying to trip and kill me." However, on Day Five, which had been so generously given to us for our unfettered enjoyment, I moaned all day long, beginning with "Where is the sun?" and ending with "I can't believe how much of a waste this day was." In between, I hated the colorful toys I saw while shopping at IKEA. I even hated pumpkins. We called this a slip.

Day Seven:

I reviewed the reason no-complaint week began. It started after I bought a small collection of witticisms called *Shit Happens, Get Over It*. It got me thinking about a new positive mantra: "Pull weeds, plant flowers." Did it work? We both said yes, it did. It was a vacation to give the bad vibes a rest and grow our personal positive gardens, weeds be damned. Day Seven was hopeful and cheery for both of us and we renewed our pact for another week to see what miraculous changes could occur.

But first we let it all hang out and had a major, full-on groan fest, no flowers, not even seedlings. I mean, what in the world are old girlfriends for?

The sin on my shoulder

When she first appeared it was shocking, unexpected, unwelcome. I was standing in a dressing room trying on a nightgown, pretending to look sexy. Then she popped up like a chipmunk or a rat, sticking her face where she didn't belong.

Despite the rolls and wrinkles already staring me down, Greta emerged as the most dominant blight in the mirror, a sudden volcanic eruption as unpredictable as Krakatoa.

Her head was round, somewhere between a blueberry and a cantaloupe. She was smooth, firm, young, enough reasons to hate her right there. And she was sitting closer to me than my own arm, perched on my clavicle like a lost demon. No warning, no shyness, only a grand entrance. Defiant, formidable, ugly as sin.

"So now that you're older," a friend said, "are things going to pop up all over your body?"

The answer is yes. Yes, they are.

Greta is a large ganglion cyst. The day was getting worse.

The habit of giving names to things—creatures, plush toys, hunks of chunky metal—follows an old human need to bond, creating a partnership so the two of you can solve the inevitable ups and downs of life. Greta is, in the physical sense, an up, though believe me, she's a downer.

Yes, maybe I'd bashed into a wall on that spot on the collarbone. And yes, maybe one day she'd be gone as quickly as she came, or maybe one day a surgeon would need to encourage her to leave.

Weeks passed; Greta stood tall.

At first, I was awed by the way she came from nowhere with the boldness of an intruder and made herself right at home.

Then I was disheartened. On warm days, how does one incorporate a humpy, hideous thing into sleeveless sheaths and unforgiving bathing suits?

How exactly do you dress a ganglion cyst?

"Why don't you name her?" my niece Barrie said on a shopping trip a month after my conjoined twin arrived. "Maybe the problem is you haven't been properly introduced."

So I named her. And the relationship truly got better. I said that only because she's listening.

For maybe a thousand years, there's evidence people have been naming inanimate objects that are critical to their lives: boats, castles, swords (*think Excalibur!*). Today, maybe computers, houses, cell phones. It's estimated 25 percent of people name their cars. I've had Goblin, my Volkswagen, and Venus, my Volvo.

Blundering

My BFF yoga mat is Sticky. And we have the Girlfriend, the snake plant Ray treats like a goddess. I even have a pocketbook named Fake; she's honest to goodness pure, cheap vinyl.

Names help us pretend things have human characteristics, so we accept their whims and fancies, believe they have minds of their own. Like when Fake bangs me in the butt when I fill her too fat. *You fake!*

Sometimes we anthropomorphize things because we love them and consider them extensions of ourselves. It helps us pretend they're watching over us, keeping us safe and sound. I imagined Goblin, for example, scared the fenders off any mechanical hunk that came close.

In the case of Greta, there's no doubt she's an extension, and there's no doubt she's close enough to watch every move, hear every whisper.

After I named her, hate didn't exactly turn into love, but it did turn into a business arrangement, as she and I went face-to-face in the mirror, as I exposed her and let the wind run across her rounded slopes, hoping she'd be pacified. And eventually I noticed her ego had been tamed. Meaning there's less of her than there once was. As quickly as she came, months later, she shrunk. Though I still see the top of her head, the whites of her eyes.

This brings up another lesson, one about impermanence. About how things come and how things go, about how nothing lasts forever, about how change is the only constant in life.

About how, as the Good Book says, "to everything there is a season." And how that season—*Greta, I'm talking to you*—is decidedly not the off-the-shoulder, let-it-hang-out summer, when certainly you can take a vacation of your own.

Greta, are you listening?

My sexy French dentist fills me up

For a memorable trip, you need a broken ankle (Granada), a buttock full of chigger bites (a Swiss lake), a bloody fall through the Alps (Italy), or a messy ailment that starts with a lovely meal that's later ejected with enough force to topple the Taj Mahal (India).

Or a broken tooth in France.

I know what you're thinking: it's a boring tooth. Well, let me repeat what a friend said: "Don't get sick in France in the summer because all the doctors are *en vacances.*"

If I'd known the doctors took the dentists with them, I'd have replaced my precious set with dentures before I went, like locking your diamond necklace in a vault and wearing a replica to the ball.

Because when my teeth aren't happy, nobody is happy on either side of the Atlantic.

The tooth cracked while sucking a Tic Tac for a fresh French *bouche.* As I slowly savored it—okay, maybe I took a hard bite out of the thing—a tiny slice of enamel slid off, becoming indistinguishable from the mint around it.

Immediately, I knew the earth's tectonic plates had shifted. Two jagged peaks like the French Alps appeared. But you couldn't hike them or ski them. You couldn't even chew them.

For all practical purposes, I was toothless.

Disasters of the past flooded in, reminding me that leaving home is one of the most idiotic things a person can do. Sure, most accidents happen at home, but at least you know who to call.

While *les dentistes* enjoyed their own crack-ups elsewhere, I dialed a dozen heartless answering machines and fought an attempt by locals to take me to the hospital because, "That's what we do in France in the summer." Finally, Dr. Jean-Francois picked up his phone and said *bonjour.*

He was, shall we say, a bit *avant-garde*, which is what you want in France, except when it comes to your teeth.

Jean-Francois had no plucky hygienist ready with water, clean utensils, and a bib. The second I walked in, a young woman walked out—maybe an assistant, maybe a patient, maybe a victim—and I became the replacement female in an office that had doors that led to more doors in a circuitous labyrinth that I feared would end in a deep dark dungeon.

One door closed behind me. I shuddered.

Monsieur Dentiste appeared in a swirl of flimsy white cloth like a sheik entering his palace. He was handsome, lithe, and I had to concede, sexy. He *was* French. He spoke enough English to make me feel he knew what I needed.

But did he know what I didn't need?

I was led into a cavernous white space capped with a lascivious mural of reds, greens, and golds. It depicted a Roman orgy, the early French sex trade, Bacchus and Venus comparing notes, or the S&M gear we would wear while I received a powerful injection that would leave me with my jaw dropping open for maybe more than one reason.

I wondered why this guy wasn't on vacation. *Did nobody love him?*

I did a mental checklist of emergency meds I had back at the hotel. Antibiotic cream, itch cream, pills for nausea, insomnia, mad cow disease. Could a Band-Aid be fashioned, I wondered, for a tooth? How about Moleskin? Yeah, how about Moleskin …

Jean-Francois, his artwork framing him in a lusty light, pronounced his diagnosis. I needed Novocain, lots of drilling, and the insertion of some new-fangled French something-or-other into my helpless mouth. A crown? An arm? His accent made him sound like a cross between Dracula, Arnold Schwarzenegger, and a used car salesman when he said, "Maybe you have deep cavity. I must fill and quickly."

I was *beaucoup* nervous.

Some bad French later, *le dentiste* and his drill looking limp, I'm relieved to say I left with no needle, no drilling, and a plop of cement covering the tiny Alps—a temporary solution until I got back to somebody with no porno on the walls.

That would be my local dentist, who now seems a bit dull if you want to know the truth. He told me the guy did such a good job I should leave it alone, which I guess makes me part French for now.

Ooh la la, Jean-Francois.

Diary of bone-chilling leisure

When was the last time you thought of peeking into someone else's diary or— the seemingly mature version—the journal? A page or two perhaps, not the things that make you cringe, just enough to get a sense of what another deranged soul is thinking first thing in the morning or last thing at night.

So here you go, a few pages from mine, to show how the human brain works when faced with a sudden, irrevocable, bone-chilling event that tips its precarious balance. Bottom line: the mind can be a kooky place to live.

Dear Diary,

Monday: Ha! How lucky was that slip. Wow! This is just a tiny twisty sprain. Beat the odds again. I can walk on this ankle great, maybe with a wince and a wiggle, but hobbling counts. I'll put some spit on it and go on with my very important day. Ouch! Well, okay, maybe I'll take a short break (*don't say break*)—Rest, Ice, Compression, Elevation, or R.I.C.E. as they say, preferably brown rice—and that'll be it. I'm fine, I'm absolutely fine. That was close. Whew!

Tuesday: So it's swollen. What isn't swollen? My eyes when I get up in the morning, my feet at the end of the day, my ego when I decide I'm stronger, smarter, and way better looking than the person near me until the next one shatters (*don't say shatter*) my cool. This is not ego talking. This is my body saying, "Not again, not another ankle"—even if it does hurt, especially if it hurts. Just testing me, is all. But it doesn't hurt, so long as I don't move it or try to move anything else. Or stand up or sit or lie down. I know! For a while, I'll just lean.

Wednesday: Alright, already, maybe I'll pay the doctor a visit so people will leave me alone. Nothing worse than so-called friends and family saying denial may be a river in Egypt, but delusion is a ticket to the Dead Sea. I guess I better get on it before they stage an intervention. I'll humor that annoying cast of characters (*don't say cast*) so I can crack the whip (*don't say crack*) sometime in the future.

Thursday: It's broken, dear Diary. I have a hairline fracture on the skinny fibula, a Robocop boot, and scary crutches. And it hurts. HELP, dear Diary, HELP …

I called feisty ninety-six-year-old Aunt Wanda who'd had at least a dozen surgeries over the years and many broken bones.

"Let me tell you," she advised, in one of her rare subdued tones, "if there's one thing I've learned about how to handle this kind of thing, it's to enjoy it."

Me: Enjoy the pain and suffering?

Wanda: Of course not. But this is one of those special

times you can rest. Don't push, pretend you're at the beach, and keep yourself entertained the best way you can. Read, watch Netflix, eat good food, let people take care of you. If there's anything I've learned in my life of injuries, it's to enjoy this time of leisure. I don't mean accept it, I don't mean tolerate it, I don't mean grin and bear it. I mean enjoy it. It can really be quite wonderful.

Me: But I've already broken six other bones, remember? This is my second broken ankle. Isn't that enough leisure already?

Wanda: What good does all that yoga do for you, anyway?

Friday: Okay, dear Diary, we have our marching orders (*yes, think march!*), so let's try to grow up and Rock-and-R.Y.C.E. the new way. Read, do Yoga lying down, Chill, and most of all, listen to your aunt and Enjoy the rest.

Wanda says, "Could it hurt?"

Get out now

In a given week, how often do you drive away from home, remember you left something on the stove or forgot your gym bag or your shopping list or the gift you're carrying to a party, and you turn back? Your neighbors see you rush out like the Mad Hatter and return crawling like a centipede, head tucked to the ground.

Her again.

You run back for hand sanitizer or tissues or dental floss. What if you need those? *What if, what if, what if?* You grab a hat and gloves should the car break down on a mountain, a snack should you find yourself starving in a forest, water if you become parched in a desert, critical phone numbers or even a phone. *Oh my God, the phone!*

You're determined to make a quick exit, start the day bursting forth, not apologize for being late again, not feel terrible about yourself. You scream, "I've got to get out of the house!"

And yet …

What if you never come back? What will the family think when face-to-face with your expired yogurt, wilting plants, messy desk? Will they think a real person lived there? Humiliating. You clean a little.

"I'm coming, I'm coming, I'm coming ..."

Or, in those last frantic minutes when you twist a wrist, brush your teeth with Comet, break a glass—do you fret the skirt you're wearing reveals your dimply thighs, or your tights will pinch or sag, or you're out of painkillers should something bleed or swell far from Rite Aid?

In which case you might need Google maps. But what if the phone is dead and where is that power cord?

"I'm coming, in a second, I'm coming ..."

To get out of the house, I take precautions. I fill my car with blankets should the temperature drop, a bathing suit should a lake come into view, a crown to greet an audience. I manage the possibilities.

Yet what if someone else is driving?

"I'm coming, I swear, I'm coming ..."

Soon. But if I wash the dishes or throw in some laundry or straighten a bookshelf, I'll be more relaxed later when I come home, even if I'm less relaxed now. Especially after banging into a door, and suddenly I have ice on my arm.

Still, I wonder, *Shouldn't I road test these shoes by taking out the trash?*

Not wanting to feel crummy about myself—*late again!*—I have an idea: start earlier. And a rationale: the time I waste in last-minute rummaging and racing, driving away, coming back, is the same block of time I could use on the front end to exit gracefully and stay out. What a novel idea.

Did you say start a novel?

Two thousand years ago, people seemed to be the same way when they tried to get up and going. I know this because the Roman poet Virgil said, "The hour is ripe and yonder lies the way."

In other words: get out now.

Virgil must have been trying to convince a drunken warrior to board the carriage, jump on the horse, grab the lance or the walking stick, and forget about plucking the grapes from the vine.

Too bad. On a long, hot journey—especially in dry, dusty, ancient Rome—I bet those grapes would have tasted pretty darn good.

The naked thief

Have you ever worried you'll lose your clothes in a dressing room while begging random shoppers for an opinion on a new outfit? Or you'll run out of the house when deer start eating your hostas and forget you're naked? Or villains from another planet will abduct you in the middle of the night and zap your nightgown, leaving your body for all to see?

Me neither. But when it comes to baring all, the imagination does tend to run wild.

Certainly, though, you have dreamed of being shamefully exposed in some fashion or another, perhaps while sitting at a meeting nude and helpless, your head tucked between your knees.

These dreams, according to psychologists, could mean a fear of embarrassment, a sense of inferiority, or a desire for attention—because naked does seem to attract a crowd.

Well, I'm glad to report I can cross the naked fear off my list. If you need to picture how this happened, imagine a petite woman with wet hair in a tiny towel looking like a pig in a blanket while bent over the floor struggling to unlock a gym locker, her hind cheeks high in the air.

Not so horrible, unless it goes on for an interminably long time, which it did, because Locker Number 350 would not open with my secret combination, 911.

After consulting a curious group of sweaty onlookers, I picked up the emergency phone in the locker room and soon my criminal interrogation began.

Attendant: Can you please tell me what's in the locker?

Me: Um, my clothes. Have you noticed my quivering flesh is totally visible top to bottom?

Attendant (dead serious): What kind of clothes?

Me: The clothes I need to cover my buck-naked butt. *Hello!*

Attendant: And what would those clothes look like? I need exact details.

Me: (Is this a joke? Who remembers these things?) Uh, um ... black sweatpants, a gray T-shirt, a baseball cap, maybe sneakers. Yes, black sneakers. What else do I ever wear? Oh, and a hazmat suit because you never know what will happen on any given day, as we're proving right now.

Satisfied, she inserts her key while I panic I've gotten the locker wrong and will soon be revealed as the naked thief I am. Glory be, my clothes are there.

Curious who would stage a snatch like this, I asked the attendant if naked people had tried to steal this way before.

Attendant: Never.

Me: I know you're trained to ask these questions but is it possible, even in your wildest naked dreams, to envision a situation in which a dripping nude female would conduct a heist of expensive streetwear in this fashion?

She listened, maybe afraid I'd gone mad and would report her.

Me: So let me see ... First, the cunning thief cases the joint, chooses a well-dressed victim, and watches her change into a lululemon outfit and Nikes. Then the thief hides her own clothes, grabs a shower, wraps herself in a mildly absorbent piece of terry cloth, and lurks in wait for the perfect moment to call security hoping they get there before the hapless victim huffs and puffs back in.

Timing is critical, I told her, and would require super-human powers of transportation to also watch the second floor StairMaster where the victim could be pumping away.

Or, thinking one can't play this caper more than once, I said it would be good if the first burglary pays off mighty well. That would demand superhuman vision to see if any money is inside a pocket inside the clothes inside the locker inside the gym.

Still, I added to my poor attendant, if it could by some miraculous feat be done, it could be worth it, because it could give a dull suburbanite and upstanding yogi a radical new identity, and who doesn't want that at some point in life?

I paused for a moment and considered whether I felt insulted or embarrassed or annoyed in any way. I didn't. Instead, I realized, I felt younger and stronger and bold, and that shocked me more than being caught with my pants gone.

I grabbed my attendant, gave her a big smile, and thanked her for making my day. Really, I told her, when was the last time anyone implied, in even the slightest way, that I had superhuman powers?

Go on, have a
hot toddy

When it comes to food, alcohol, caffeine, dust—anything solid or liquid that goes in or near the body, anything that flies by or drips down—my family members have a reaction. We get food poisoning, sea sickness, air sickness, rashes.

When one of us travels we ask, "How'd it go?" We don't mean did you have fun or great adventures? In my family, we mean did you embarrass yourself in front of friends, strangers? Did you have to disguise yourself in a hat and mustache?

For example, one wimpy relative had to receive oxygen on a flight after overdosing on a PowerBar. Disappointing, because PowerBars have now been added to our substances banned in public, reducing our choices to water and Gerber's squash.

So, with wimpy ancestry, I made a fuss when it was suggested I try a hot toddy for a cold. I've never had an official hot toddy. No whiskey at all since falling dead drunk one night on a single Irish whiskey in my twenties. I had no desire to again be dragged from a bar while dressed in hot pink, thrown into a car, and relocated to my bed where I stayed for three days. I even lost an earring.

Nope, once was enough. And yet ...

With everyone around complaining of some cough or sneeze, including me, I figured no better time to test if I could manage an old-fashioned home remedy without impacting every man, woman, and child in the Mid-Atlantic.

I picked up the idea from the massage therapist who was working on the stiff neck I got from coughing. A hot toddy, he said, is his secret weapon against clients who give him the sniffles. As soon as day is done, he runs home, mixes hot tea with lemon, honey, and a good shot of bourbon. "I shiver it out," confided Joe. "It works every time, and it makes me feel really, really good."

The closest I've ever gotten to such a brew is a *gogol-mogol*, and it made me feel really, really bad. This unpalatable Russian tonic was Mom's super cure for sore throats, a disgusting blend of hot milk, eggs, butter, and honey we kids were forced to guzzle. This is why none of us can barely ingest a single thing.

Maybe it was time to grow up.

I decided to give the toddy the old hot pink try. I searched for the perfect recipe. I wanted the full ancient treatment in honor of the Scots who perhaps invented the concoction hundreds of years ago. Maybe in the middle of some fiery war with nothing but charred toads to snack on. The name must have changed in translation.

Blundering

But first I asked a nurse.

Me: Does a hot toddy work?

Nurse: Well, I don't know if it will heal you, but it won't do you any harm.

She didn't know my family.

I went with this recipe:

- 1 wimpy shot of whiskey
- 2 lemon slices
- 5 whole cloves
- Hot tea (decaf for me)
- Cinnamon stick

I put the tea bag in a cup with the lemon slices skewered with cloves, added the other ingredients, and topped it all with boiling water. Then I added a warm blanket, a good book, and a cozy couch. I thought about taking a few days off from work, but decided I wasn't feeling so bad. The hot toddy was working already.

I lay there for a very long time. I did not wear pink. But suddenly I noticed an earring was missing.

Layer Two:
Tolerating

One day you look in the mirror and think you look fabulous—a hallucination?—and the next day you refuse to go out of the house. It's like that at the computer, too. One day you delude yourself into thinking you're a writing phenom, and the next day you can't pen a grocery list.

In the yoga studio, same thing. One day you keep all the moving parts together as you prepare for *adho mukha vrksasana*, the face-down tree or handstand. And the next day, your feet are glued to the ground and your arms are shaking.

So you try again. You go near a wall, put your hands on the floor, straighten your arms, lift your hips, walk in. Then you command yourself to JUMP UP so you can balance upside down on the wall. You imagine yourself as the grounded and growing, tall and stalwart, graceful and long-lasting tree.

You topple.

When you wonder what happened from one day to the next—from the mirror to the computer to the studio, after judging yourself, berating yourself, rejecting yourself—most of the time you can't find an answer. And finally, you decide to laugh at yourself because all the other emotions have already been spent.

Yet slowly, you make progress. You realize that showing up for your daily yoga practice gives you the clarity to finish a story or balance without keeling over. And you somehow finesse the latest body dysmorphia meltdown with greater ease, more tolerance, and more ability to control your inner turmoil.

Unless you do something dangerous like shop for a pair of jeans.

Mid-rise jeans for midlife women

Are you comfortable in your jeans?

I'm not asking a profound question like, "Are you comfortable in your skin?" I'm asking a question as superficial as pancake makeup.

Are you comfortable wearing the only pants that look fashionable through a relaxing family breakfast, a power lunch, a sexy, romantic dinner? You know, the usual trajectory of your average woman's day.

Personally, I'm tired of pretending. I confessed to a friend that my low-rise jeans can no longer go from morning 'til night. Like me, they're distressed, and not in a stonewashed way. They've been too yanked up, and I've been doing the yanking.

Low-rise jeans have taken the fight out of me and my pants.

My friend, speaking in a whisper, shared my misery. Then she grabbed her tight blues so she could walk without revealing the cleft between the two protruding lumps wiggling behind her.

Or the way-too-much-information issue in the way-down front. Her jeans were as low as a hip-hopper, and she was forced to awkwardly pull up with her hands as she pushed forward with her feet, multitasking while making a simple run to the ladies' room.

What's a woman with a body to do?

For starters, don't discuss the issue with anyone younger than thirty.

"Waists are no longer in," said my friend's eleven-year-old daughter. "Straight is in, waists are out." Then she pursed her lips, put her hands on her hips, and posed like an underage stripper. She explained that low-rise prevents a sloppy break anywhere near the waist—that dreaded muffin top—keeping things neater, leaner.

It was refreshing to know that soon enough she and her friends would think they were fat.

I was so amazed by this preteen news, I made a beeline to Nordstrom. If waists were out, and I happen to have one, I was hoping to grab old-fashioned rejects on a sale rack. Or maybe there would be a protest I could join.

Thankfully, that nymphette was wrong. Super low-rise jeans, I learned, are out for true women because they made everyone above eleven miserable. What's available for us more seasoned sex kittens—and that changes daily—are mid-rise jeans. But don't get too excited. They've added maybe a millimeter. They're still low-rise jeans with "mid" in the name to make middle-aged women buy more of them.

"They're still too low?" groaned my twenty-something saleswoman, looking at me with raw pity though I was thinner than her, had less protrusion between my navel and that exposed secret place, and, I swore, she would never look as good as I do at my age.

Fortunately, I *am* my age, so I managed to smile and only barely wiggle my butt at her when she went to grab more brands for me to try. "You will never shake like this," I said under my breath as I yanked up my jeans.

I eventually sampled every pair in the store, while she checked in.

"How you doin'?" she fretted, frowning like I was a social work project. She managed to leave off the "hun," though I could hear it in her voice.

"We wouldn't be in this mess," I explained as the wiser woman, "if blue jeans were made for real genes."

"But they're so comfortable," she mewed.

"Oh, come on, hun," was all I could say.

Were we ever comfortable in our jeans? When I was young like her, I remember wearing nothing but jeans day in, day out. I also slept on floors, forgot to eat, and thought a fun time was hanging out with a couple of girlfriends and seeing if any guys showed up. Today that would ruin a wonderful girls' night out.

But I swear there was a time my jeans never pinched, sagged, needed washing, or exposed the entire circumference of my midsection to within one inch of being arrested. They got better the longer I wore them, especially if I sat on a curb to wait for a bus or took a snooze on a lawn between classes.

Yes, it's a dirty little secret: No matter how much we love them, the older we get, the worse our jeans feel. I say we throw the bums out.

P.S. "Hun" sold me two new pairs.

The skinny on skin

S ince I've decided to take better care of my aging skin, I have no time left to go anywhere to show it.

The regimen recommended by my esthetician, Veruschka (say that five times to stretch your face), goes like this:

After a good cleanse, start your daily routine with three or four drops of Vitamin C patted from crown to chin. Follow with SPF 30 sunscreen, a layer of hydrating hyaluronic acid (say it five times), a dab of bleaching cream on age spots that discreetly appear on the tip of your nose, and eye balm beneath the brow and lower lid to prevent crepiness. This looks something like French crepes but, believe me, tastes nothing like them.

Immediately start drinking the first of eight daily glasses of water, then hurry out at 6 a.m. for a brief puff of air before the evil vampire of your youth rises from the east and sucks at your skin.

"I hate the sun," said Veruschka, the color of a vampire herself. "I just hate it."

The above routine is the short one. You also need a weekly deep moisturizing mask that goes where no man has gone before, and a few morning scrubs with a FOREO, the electronic device that whirls over your scaly pores. If you're too cheap to buy one, use glycolic acid instead to slough—but never rough—away pesky flakes.

Have a nice, dark, waterlogged day. Remember to quickly wash off powder, rouge, eye makeup, lipstick, soot, grime, crumbs, sprinkles, and other people's germs. They fester on your face.

Now it's time for your evening routine, which begins at 4 p.m. or you'll be dabbing straight through 'til morning. Start with a cleanse and Retin-A, that modern medicinal that sits on your skin fifteen minutes before being covered with a thick cream with more hyaluronic acid, more bleach for spots, more eye gel.

Your gel, if you read the fine print, should be applied in a circular motion from the inside to the outside around the eye socket because everybody wants an "innie" not an "outie." Wait, wrong body part!

By now you may be hungry. Do not choose pizza, meat, salt, sugar, vegetables, fruit, or nuts, all of which make your eyes puffy, demanding another routine. I'll explain later when we reach the middle of the night because it fits in perfectly there.

Now it's time to get your beauty rest, not that you'll have any because you must lie on your back propped up on pillows without rolling side-to-side or—*holy crepiness*—onto your belly. Rolling triggers wrinkle alarms that could go off later at your son's wedding.

Since you can't sleep, head to the kitchen to prepare the puffy eye concoction you apply in the early hours to compensate for eating anything at all.

The brew consists of ice-cold cucumber slices and skim milk. Models like Gisele Bundchen maybe do this, so Veruschka was told. Hollywood actresses do it, too, except maybe Judi Dench, who won an Academy Award. She had time to work.

Brew in hand, place yourself on a plastic tarp, lie still, apply. Wait as your eyes become cucumber juleps with a little milk chaser on the side. Leave on ten minutes. Sip bourbon separately through a straw to dull the sense of curdling in your sockets.

Suddenly, it occurred to me ... *When will I have time to brush my teeth? Take my vitamins?* The rest of my body is going to rot.

Veruschka: What drives me crazy is people who spend all this money for Botox and fillers then use nothing but soap. Plain soap!

Me: So you think these toner-plumper-shrinker-tightener things really work?

Veruschka: How old do you think I am?

Me: Ummm ... twenty-one?

Veruschka: No, really. Take a guess.

Me: (timidly) Late forties?

Veruschka: (triumphantly) I'm almost fifty! (As if I was nowhere close.)

Me: Ummm ... So you think they work?

Veruschka: The truth is, at some point everything falls apart. Sags, bags, drags. Then you get a facelift.

Me: Ummm ... Wanna grab a slice of pizza?

If the shoe fits,
you're ugly

This story is not a metaphor for a deep spiritual subject like finding your rightful path or winning your ideal mate, though both would be helpful, and I'd like to read it. Instead, it's a down-and-dirty self-help primer on how to walk without pain and suffering on this scorched earth.

If you know a more worthy topic, count yourself lucky. You may not need a *pedorthist*. A what?

Not a podiatrist. Not a paleontologist. Not a psychiatrist. A *pedorthist*.

Pedorthist is the scientific name for a person who measures, molds, and modifies shoes so you can fit into a pair of six-inch heels and strut like a *pavo cristatus*, a peacock.

But if your arches are aching and your toes are curling, you may need Melvin, the official pedorthist I met at Tip Top Shoes on New York's Upper West Side.

We're talking about a problem that's baffled scientists since Caesar first asked, "Can I get a chariot, please?"

Tip Top is where I venture when my flat plates slap the ground with barely a sole or a soul separating them from hell. I used to think the expression "If the shoe fits, wear it" *was* a metaphor. Now I know it's all about shoes.

On one occasion, I dragged along a friend who has "high architecture" feet, a fancy way of saying high arches. I have low architecture. She also has bunions, and when I announced this, Melvin accused me of "globalizing" the fact because she is five foot eight and I push five foot three, but we wear the same shoe size, and I am jealous.

I noted her feet were wide and mine were narrow, the difference between tortillas and bread sticks. I pointed at her girth and cackled, anything to divert attention from the elephant feet I'd carried into the room.

Melvin was very scientific. He uses a shoehorn to fit people then instructs them like they're the first people on earth to take these shaky steps.

Melvin: One, when you put on a shoe you tap your heel toward the back and when you do, you're allowing your heel to fit into the heel counter, and two, you're allowing the architecture of your foot to line up with the congruence of the shoe, and three, you're allowing more foot movement in the toe box area and four, when you lace up the shoe think of a baby and give those laces a hug so when you're walking the foot and shoe move as one.

Me: Do you have that memorized?

Melvin: I know this stuff because I teach this stuff and because of me you're going to become a better shoe shopper. I'm going to help you understand your feet.

Me: You're going to help me become a peacock?

Melvin: Yes.

No, he didn't say that. That would be *pseudologia fantastica,* pathological lying. Instead, Melvin grabbed the most gigantic black sneaker in the joint, placed it on my skinny sticks, and announced a perfect fit. It was.

I sailed around the store bouncing and smiling. I floated down aisles hopping past bunions, jumping over stubby toes, sliding under high arches.

I was nimble as a *struthio camelus,* an ostrich. And I looked like one, too. Not a peacock, an ostrich. It's an ugly bird.

Did the shoe fit? Yes. Would I wear it outside? No. Did I buy it? Yes. As an indoor treat for my feet when they manage to get through a scorched earth day without torturing me like a scientific pedorthist faced with a wannabe pavo cristatus trying to avoid a psychiatrist.

Uber, anyone?

Omar Sharif and me

F ew people ask my age anymore. It's like a bag of Orville Redenbacher's in the microwave. There's a whole lot of activity at one point in the cycle, then things slow down, and the question gets popped only now and again. Nobody wants to get burned going anywhere near the final kernel.

Yet when my birthday comes, I still want to be spoiled rotten. I prefer the day begin with banana walnut pancakes and end on a distant planet in an unknown galaxy.

I don't even accept that other people share my day. It's mine, all mine. Statistics, of course, prove me delusional. There's a one in 365 chance the handsome guy sitting next to me at the café also dropped to earth on April 10. If there are seven billion people in the world, and 365 potential birthdays on the calendar, nineteen million people could conceivably share my sacred holiday. All of them, I hope, living in China or India.

If you up the stakes from one handsome guy to a group of twenty-three of them, there's a fifty percent chance two hot dudes will share my birthday. In a group of seventy, that shoots up to nearly one hundred percent.

I was never interested in meeting any of these con men. Until I learned that one was the drop-dead gorgeous actor Omar Sharif, and he was coming to town.

I was working as a news reporter and Sharif was in a holding room for an interview. With my twenty-five-year-old bravado, I burst into the room, my hand outstretched, and announced our bond. He seemed as shocked as I was that anyone could share his day. He rose to his feet, said "Really?" a couple of good, long times, then clasped my hands. Two partners in this very exclusive club reserved for the if-not-currently, then soon-to-be rich and famous.

So it came as a surprise one tenth of April, as I basked in the glow of the special bond between Omar and me, that the Beatles version of the "Birthday" song played in the middle of my appetizer. I was on the island of Antigua, acting spoiled in a fancy French hideaway, wondering why they started the song so early. Maybe in this part of the world they didn't wait for cake and candles.

To my amazement, another woman in the tiny restaurant of six occupied tables stood to receive her adulation. I swallowed my pride, infused myself with a dose of maturity, and traversed the restaurant to share our link.

I hid my disappointment; we communed.

Then shockingly, in the middle of my entree, the song played again, and yet another woman had the nerve to beam at yet another table. Now we were three birthday princesses in this tiny room on this tiny island in this tiny corner of the world. Forget all the people in China or India.

These other women were making my exclusive club seem as big as the Caribbean.

And I wondered, did this happen to Omar? Did anyone dare share his spotlight?

And then—in a coincidence as watered down as my frozen mojito with its drooping umbrella, and as powerful a depressant as my age—yet another woman, I swear it, received a couple of bars of the Beatles. Four birthdays out of six tables in little Antigua. All the women, except me, were barely old enough to drink.

Forced to face my comeuppance head on, I decided to try a different tack to help me feel special. I raised my wilting drink and toasted the famous birthday celebrant I knew personally who had me beaten, hands down, in the age department.

"Happy Birthday, my dear Omar, wherever you are," I said. "May you keep going until the last kernel has popped, and may I follow very, very far behind you."

For some spoiled rotten reason—I can only blame the island rum—that made me feel not just special, but young, all over again.

Doppelgänger

"You've lost half an inch" is not an expression you ever want to hear. Not if you're a seamstress, a worm, a carpenter, a tightrope walker. Not if you're a vertically challenged woman trying to puff up every measly feather she has.

I argued with the nurse. "There must be something wrong with your ruler ... I didn't stand up straight ... I'm having a slumpy day ... Are you sure you don't need glasses?" I tried it all.

Then I went home, got out the tape measure, stood tall as a light saber, and fixed myself against the height wall we keep for kids in the family. No matter how I puffed myself up, telepathically extending every hair on my squat head, my mere five foot three had shrunk closer to five foot two, and people have been calling me shrimp more than ever.

Shrimp, elf, hobbit, half-pint. Better, at least, than half-wit.

It's better, no doubt, than lots of other rude awakenings. Still, it's a mystery where that fraction of verticality went. A normal collapse in the spine perhaps, in the muscles, the tissues. Or did I inadvertently lose that length and forget where I left it, another great advantage of aging?

I have lots of perky answers when people note my dwindling: "I'm keeping the ground warm ... Don't step on me ... I'd like a kids' meal, please." One friend tried to pick me up. Hilarious. Another wrapped his arms around me, glared at the top of my head, and asked, "Why are you so short?" Ha! ... So funny, so original.

It's the kind of welcome remark I get all the time without hardly trying.

So, on behalf of all petites angling for a seat with a view, hemming every dress, straining to reach the rice on the top shelf—I decided to try harder. Here's what I came up with: *doppelgängers*.

I'll explain.

Some of the most beautiful, capable, desirable women in the world are equally challenged when it comes to stature. We don't know it, perhaps, because we see them in movies, on TV, where everything is unreal.

I'd rather be their equals in money, fame, and talent, yet I'm satisfied if they simply boost our brand. Especially after reading new evidence that doppelgängers, or lookalikes, truly exist and may share some of our DNA.

With all you lovely Lilliputians out there in mind, I'm thus taking a leap of faith and pointing a finger at a list of possible doppelgängers who could be our secret twins.

If you're a blue-eyed blonde, maybe it's Reese Witherspoon, a miniscule five foot one. Are your eyes hazel? Maybe your twin is Lady Gaga, same height as tiny Reese. We're not sure what Gaga's real hair color is, but now we know why she wears those nine-inch heels.

More on the brunette side? How about five-foot-two Eva Longoria, named one of the most beautiful women in the world. Or sexy Zoe Kravitz, Eva's same small height. Or dancing Paula Abdul, an even five-foot tall. Or shakin' five-two Shakira from Columbia, whose hips don't lie, so why should we about our height, our weight, our age? Though not telling is surely different than lying.

Every time I see myself next to giants in a mirror or photo, I can't believe it's me. I peer into the image with squinty eyes, my mouth agape, my tongue hanging. Who is that little bitty person? I'm stunned.

Kim Kardashian, also five-two, doesn't feel that way. She adores looking at herself and maybe we should, too. If you're dark-haired, brown-eyed, full-lipped, and full-bottomed, perhaps your doppelgänger is billionaire Kim. She'll be shorter when she's older. Just saying.

Think your lookalike is brainy? Ruth Bader Ginsberg topped out at five-one. Love your history? Cleopatra, a real man killer, was an even five. Athletic? Consider Simone Biles at just four-eight. Attracted to science? How about five-foot tall Madam Curie, the first woman to win a Nobel Prize.

All of us, it seems, have these unknown copies, likely more than one. Now all we need to do is find them, adopt them, brag about them, adore them, marvel at them. They're us!

Prove it otherwise.

The next time someone decides my height is so funny, I'll propose my doppelgänger Gaga would disagree. She may not be the perfect twin, but I do have hazel eyes like her, although—*I'll gently note*—I'm a full inch taller than she is. One whole full inch taller.

Ha!

Don't fake it, don't bake it

At a certain time of year, people tell me I look great. Healthy, well-rested, happy, and even ten years younger. I bask in the glow of this sudden spike in attractiveness, receiving rave reviews with just the right amount of blushing confidence.

Then I raise my head and thank the stars. One star, really, the big blazing Helios that occupies the throne at the center of our solar system, the beautiful ball of fire that drapes a glowing sheen over our drab bodies, turning us into radiant suns all our own.

Getting a tan may be one of the worst things you can do. But honestly, would you rather be greeted with "You look like a bronzed goddess" or "Are you sure there's nothing terribly wrong with you?"

At the risk of sounding like my brain is fried and I don't know about the dangers, let me confess I prefer the former. Especially when I haven't slept all night, a massive tree branch has fallen on my house, and I'm limping because of a sprained knee. Bronzed goddess is a tough act to follow on a day like that.

It's not just me. Everywhere I go—despite all the downsides—I hear tanned babes getting compliments that put still more color on their cheeks. Only Mom and the dermatologist spout the full hideous truth: the tan you get today will be the dried-out skin, the permanent sunspots, the premature wrinkles, and maybe something far worse tomorrow. No one says, "You look like a 157-year-old leatherback turtle."

When I was younger, people didn't know the sun giveth and the sun taketh away. In my teens, I used metallic reflectors to entice old Sol in my direction, and even earlier, as a toddler, my parents laid me on the sand like a little solar panel to soak up Vitamin D so I wouldn't die young, just ugly.

Today, to compensate for the damage done and the damage yet to come, while still inspiring a compliment or two, I straddle the two worlds of health and beauty.

Here's a partial list of the sunscreens in my closet: Coppertone SPORT, Banana Boat Light as Air, Blue Lizard, California Baby, Neutrogena Pure & Free, and Aveeno Absolutely Ageless.

But sometimes they block a little too much and make you look like chalk. So in no time, "I never realized how much you look like Posh Spice" becomes "Is everything really okay?"

To balance this out, I open my wallet for fake creams to give me the lush look without the leather. The list includes

Tolerating

Bobbi Brown Sunless Tanning Gel, Bare Escentuals Faux Tan, Clarins Delicious Self Tanning Cream, and St. Tropez Self Tan Classic. One makes you a bit orange, another a bit bright red, another makes you smell like a piña colada.

Back in Victorian times, high society people kept their windows tightly covered so no tiny patch of tanned skin would imply they earned money working the fields. Then, in the Roaring Twenties, a trendsetter in France—an international *it girl*—got sunburned by mistake and a new fad was born. Her name was Coco Chanel and the rest, including this mouthful—Chanel Soleil Identité Perfect Colour Face Self Tanner—is history.

One-hundred-year-old history, I might add. Coco made her rosy-cheeked discovery back in 1923. Not even gummy bears have stood that test of time.

This is all a roundabout way of saying we've been way overdue for a new trend to surpass the modern logic of preventing a real tan, getting a fake tan, preventing a real tan, and so on. We know a whole lot more than we did when Coco walked off that yacht in the French Riviera and gave women a new reason to suffer for the sake of beauty.

The new trend accepts we love the sun—we just plain love it and we're going outside!—but we must avoid "You have the veneer of a tasty California prune" or "Cowhide has nothing on you." Instead, we must again covet "Although you appear to suck blood, you have extra money to spend on your next vacation."

To where? Well, the beach of course. But this time

armed with one of those newfangled pop-up tents—another *it* thing—that blocks the view of the ocean for all the poor commoners sitting behind you, but protects you and yours inside your own fancy bubble.

Victorian times, all over again.

Dancing tips for babes

When everything gets you down—the bills, your health, the kids, your friends—take that pent up energy and use it in the best way human beings can to instantaneously turn killer tension into awesome talent. All without needing special equipment, a new outfit, a note from your doctor, a prescription, an advanced degree, a hidden motel room, or even a willing partner.

Go on. Loosen up. Dance. Who cares?

The way I see it, you can break into a full-on dance move anywhere—Walmart, the car wash, the coffee shop, the office—and no one will begrudge you. Instead, they'll thank you for turning another dull day into an opportunity to revel in the human spirit.

Or is this all about me?

Am I another geeky version of Elaine from *Seinfeld* who did a combo move of Irish jig and desperate hitchhiker that made even Kramer wince? Or worse yet, am I that embarrassing aunt at a family wedding?

I think I might be that aunt.

Because at a particular family bar mitzvah, you wouldn't know boogying was good for you at all. Within minutes of starting to shake it up with thirteen-year-olds, I was put on notice by a teenage cousin that I wasn't doing it "right."

I'll tell you who cares if you let down your hair. Young people. Everything we do is mortifying.

While I attempted to boogie, this horrified beauty rolled her head, bugged her eyes, and made horizontal slicing movements with her hands to indicate I should cease and desist immediately. She did all this ever so slightly because she didn't want to draw any attention to *herself*. I felt as up to date as a coin-operated telephone.

I was *that* aunt.

Now look, I consider myself a fairly good dancer. Delusional? Possibly. But in my defense, which I will mount at this time, I've even won some dance contests stomping, mashing, sliding, and kicking. No, it wasn't *Dancing with the Stars,* and maybe I'm no Beyoncé, but I can do a pretty mean booty shake.

And I've been the star of a dance video. Okay, maybe it was shot by Ray on a deserted beach when he caught me tearing up the sand with my iPod and my favorite *World Groove* album, which I challenge anyone to hear without rockin' out.

But I swear I did not enter this boring bar mitzvah dance floor with one finger stuck in the air á la John Travolta in *Saturday Night Fever,* though if you can find me a better dance movie, I'll buy you popcorn that costs a quarter. Instead, I was doing my updated female version of spastic-to-smooth á la James Brown with some Michael Jackson heel grooving and Jennifer Lopez hair shaking without the Jennifer Lopez hair.

Eat your heart out, Rhianna.

But no budding Shakiras or Ushers were found at this party. The kids weren't really dancing at all. The boys were jumping up and down as if evading a man-eating crocodile while pumping their fists in the air ready to foment revolution before inhaling pigs in a blanket and Sprite and waiting for their parents to pick them up.

The girls moved. A little. A few mini booty shakes and equally mini fist pumps.

Come on, girls, do not under any circumstances give in to the boys on the dance floor. As time goes on, most of them will refuse to dance at all while you will cut a rug with your girlfriends. Now is the time to show them up.

Not to be upstaged, and piqued after the event, I decided to update my own dance moves by watching YouTube. I found the so-called Groove Walk, or "It's Your Move, It's Your Body, It's Your Groove."

I'll try to explain this. First you do a mini walk, then a body roll by pushing out your chest and butt. Come on! Chest, butt, chest, butt! Then add an elbow pop with your elbows jutting to the side, then "party with your arms"— you know what I mean—then sleek down your own hair like a partner caressing you. It's best if your mouth is somewhat open, suggesting willingness.

Next, it seems, the cool dancer can move on to advanced grinding, which excuse me please, lovely children, was invented before any of you were even twinkles in your great, great, great, great grandparents' eyes. *You're kidding me, right?*

Move over Generation Z. And when you do, at least try to shake it.

Blue nail polish

When a woman has an issue, she consults her girl-friends. And girlfriends can be quite opinion-ated unless you let them know you're not, NOT, asking them to fix it.

All you want is a sounding board, someone to let you talk freely of the pros and cons, the what ifs or why nots, the fears and frets, so you can move on and make your own bad decision you'll live to regret.

But you know friends. They're chewing their lips and veins are bulging out of their necks and foam is escaping from their mouths because they're desperate to solve your problem so they don't have to solve one of their own.

Wouldn't it be nice to let them have a go at it? Just for once, like a vacation from yourself, let someone else decide if you should make the phone call, sign on the dotted line, book the hotel, take the job, marry the man.

People adore helping people make decisions; that's what the experts say. But there's a catch: They don't want to be deciders, they want to be advisors. Like the difference between getting on a plane and dropping someone off at departures.

I need people to come along for the flight.

But after weeks of debating one nagging issue, my friends were not willing. I pushed them further. "East, south, west, Venus, I don't care," I yelled. "Just tell me what to do. I've given up the fight."

I decided to pester eighteen people. That's an exaggeration. Not the number but the suggestion that I decided anything. I didn't. It was just that the first seventeen people didn't have the faintest idea what they were talking about, so I added one more. She didn't know what she was talking about, either, but I prefer even numbers.

I also asked eighteen people because I wanted consensus; I didn't want resentment should I follow one person's crummy advice. I was protecting my friends and the new acquaintances who happened to be standing in the deli line when I grabbed lunch. Lunch is a good place to find strangers with no quick response to "Got an hour?"

Yet even those poor souls who could say any crazy thing—"Sure, sure, become a bank robber"—cracked midway through "Yeah, but" and "Easy for you to say." Even when I pushed—"Tell me what to do and I swear I'll do it"—they acted like I was violating that old adage, "You can't put your head on someone else's shoulders."

People can be so rigid!

Finally, with no one willing to take my life in their hands, I came to this: Give them all another chance. Maybe they were busy with their own messes. Be magnanimous, be forgiving. I wouldn't get to most of them anyway, because soon the decision would kill me.

You may be curious what I was deciding. No life-or-death matter, not at all, though you wouldn't have known by my fetal position. I was trying to go on a yoga retreat alone and join a fun family excursion at the same time.

Why are the truly tough questions like these—or whether to buy the blue or purple nail polish—so much harder than the frivolous ones?

Desperate, I re-called the first person on my list to re-pose the options. By then I assumed she would have forgotten the whole sordid thing because she has a life. We could start fresh. I was wrong. Before I even launched, she screamed, "Just do it or don't do it. Will it really matter ten years from now?"

Hmmm ... I'll have to get back to you on that one.

What an octopus knows

A re you enthralled with the octopus?

If you're a woman of a certain age ready to buy new clothes, you may want to keep that mollusk in mind before you have a conversation that goes something like this:

Me: Do my arms still look good in sleeveless, or am I done?

Loaded words aimed at my friend Noelle at a boutique as the warmth wafted in and thoughts of cool tank tops floated on the wind.

Noelle (thoughtful, sensitive, scared to death): Uhhh ...

Me (pleading my case): I do yoga, I swim, I lift weights.

I couldn't win a tussle with a 600-pound giant Pacific octopus—the biggest on record—but I haven't gained weight, I haven't lost it. There's no reason, I said, these arms should be less capable since I last asked that question, maybe the year before.

Noelle (avoiding direct eye contact): At least you're not an octopus. You'd have eight arms. That's a lot of jiggly flesh.

This didn't sound promising.

The octopus was on the tip of many tongues after a creature named Inky escaped from his tank at a New Zealand aquarium, slithered to an open drainpipe, and dropped into the waiting sea, making him an international star.

This ramped up public obsession about these once scary monsters. Noelle, who happens to be from New Zealand, is tickled with her cunning soulmate. My niece Molly is also besotted. She's hoarded octopuses her whole life: stuffed animals, key chains, knickknacks, necklaces. She once lost her favorite plush pink octopus Beanie Baby, also named Inky, and still considers this the moment she left her carefree childhood behind.

Like her, many of us love the bizarre octopus and every one of its capable arms. Fabulously smart yet funny looking, octopuses explore every inch of their worlds. They can solve puzzles, use tools, commune with humans—all with their twisting, tenacious, terribly talented tentacles.

Much like us.

But Inky and his fellow cephalopods also have arm suckers, hundreds and hundreds of them, that taste and cling, and arms that change color quicker than we can try on a strapless bandeau. They can easily hide from prey, while we can only pray we're stronger than what's chasing us. One of their slimy limbs also has sex organs if they're male, making things very convenient if they're concerned about having a long enough reach.

And best of all for Inky, his arms can regenerate, become young and new all over again, something we'd give up more than tank tops for.

I stared at my puny appendages. They were not Inky class, but they could lift and crawl and reach and carry and hug and haul and help eat and groom.

Me: So you're saying my arms look jelly-ish and crepey?

Noelle (turning away): Did you know octopus arms still move when they're severed from the body?

I could relate. The skin of my arms has become ever so faintly unattached from the muscle beneath it. But still, I can snag a fish, so long as it's lying on a plate.

I glanced in the mirror and reflected on Inky. He made it all the way out to sea with those arms. He escaped the limits of his cage. What would he say, if he could, about my tank top dilemma?

With warm winds brushing my naked skin, with the carefree days of summer beckoning and beguiling, and with me fretting my limbs weren't as nimble and nubile as they used to be, I bet he'd tell me to escape my self-imposed cage and let nature envelop my bare, amazing arms.

Fryes or Uggs?

The boot is the badass brother to the flip flop. I realized this as I stacked the flimsy rubber thongs in the closet and dragged down the massive boots, old and worn. Flip flops are like sponges on your feet, wiping up the floor. Boots are like shop vacs, powerful enough to wipe out your enemy.

The boot army was weak; I needed reinforcements. I called Zappos.

Riddle: Why didn't the sun go to college?

Answer: Because it already had a million degrees.

That's how the shoe company answers the phone, by offering a joke of the day. You need it when faced with 4,784 choices for boots, three of which will fit.

"A boot is a very versatile shoe," said Irene, my Zappos saleswoman. "Years ago, boots were sturdy things you wore for snow. Now they're everyday hip. Everything has changed."

Yet when I asked what brand might be super solid and also kick some fashion butt, I was directed to the boot I wore as a teenager: Frye.

"Everybody wants Fryes and Uggs," she said. "They fly off the shelves."

Fryes are expensive, but according to Irene, they're worth three pairs of lesser boots. We sat on the phone as I scanned styles online and learned what every hard-to-fit woman needs to know, details about shaft height and width, something I thought we cared about for a different reason. All the talk about street walking had put my mind in the gutter.

We laughed, another joke while boot shopping.

The shaft is the part of the shoe from the ankle to the top. You don't worry about it unless the shaft is so high you can barely bend your knee, which is what happens to me because of my height: I walk like a zombie. That's because my legs are no longer considered normal length. These days, petite is not considered "in."

"It's the chemicals we eat," offered Irene. "Women keep getting taller and fuller. We used to sell out of size sevens immediately. Now it's size nines and tens."

I imagined a future generation of female titans inhabiting the earth, fashionably pounding the pavement, delivering the world from ugly and evil.

The shaft width, meantime, is the part of the boot that goes around the calf, and again Irene had something to add: "Women are fitter than they used to be, more athletic, more muscles, so calf width is getting bigger."

I pictured not just tall but brawny, colossal lady avengers, decimating the pavement, calves bashing side to side into cars, buildings, planets. All while looking mighty fightin' fabulous. I wanted this, any way I could get it.

Yet little by little, as we worked through dimensions, my choices narrowed like the width of my feet. They don't make narrow widths much anymore and that's what I need.

"What about us smaller people?" I asked. "We can't just go in and out of vogue like gladiator sandals or platform shoes."

We laughed again.

Irene explained boots are more popular than regular shoes in the cool months, and completely cool in another way when it's warm.

"Boots work with everything," she explained. "Skirts, dresses, business, casual. A low boot goes terrific with a dress or a business suit. It's a great look. The women here at Zappos, no matter how old, love to wear shorts with their Fryes."

I asked if there was an age limit to boots with shorts, or even boots with bikinis, then pictured aging goliaths stomping around Zappos with barely a thing above the knees but a fierce power below them.

"It's not about your age," said Irene. "It's about your style and attitude."

"Then again," she revealed, "I live in Las Vegas."

Riddle: What do boot lovers say at breakfast?

Answer: Frye me an Ugg.

Mirror, mirror
on the wall

A self-talk recommendation on my daily affirmation calendar was this: "Every time I pass a mirror, I say out loud, 'Hi, honey' and wave."

You can imagine what the scene was like at my house after following along, with Ray thinking I was cozying up to him when I was just sugar-coating myself, and with him being curious if a screw had loosened.

My house, like yours perhaps, is filled with mirrors room-to-room, floor-to-ceiling, lying in wait behind doors, bursting with light at the bottom of stairs, so I can routinely—okay obsessively—check how bad things are. Then I attempt any necessary repairs, which are always far short of the goal and often make me leave the scene of the affront with a sigh, not a wink and a wave.

All that has changed, though, because my affirmation calendars have been guiding my attitudes and behaviors for many a long day, many a successive year. Without a daily reminder to be upbeat—to envision a life more peaceful, empowered, and utopian—who knows how a year would transpire. Who knows how often the word shouted at that fickle mirror, mirror on the wall would be "Witch, witch, witch."

Yet with age ascending even as newer styles reveal all— the wrinkles, the pouches, the cellulite—I'm reminded a little honey could go a long way toward making life a little sweeter. I mean, what can you do about the fact that your thighs, despite your best fitness efforts, and your belly, despite living on sugar-free this and fat-free that, continue to fight you? What can you do about the fact you were born who you are, which you're still working to accept, affirmation by affirmation, like this one from the calendar: "My life gets more fabulous every day."

Says who?

For that day, at least, says me.

But the mirror strategy still leaves me besotted. *What a great idea,* I think, as I pass the reflecting glass and note how often I ruin an otherwise good day by sabotaging myself with ridicule: *Oh yeah, you look like you slept on a bus.* Or, *Oh yeah, better grab that hat and sunglasses before anyone recognizes you.*

So much nicer, I must admit, and so much more gracious to give a nod, a thumbs up, a "Hi, honey," and a fluttery wave each time the mirror hits me smack in the marionette lines.

I love you, honey!

An old friend once said the trick to having a good day is to take the last look in the morning into a mirror that does you justice. The one with the best lighting, perhaps with a soft candle nearby, that makes you feel somehow young and beautiful. *I am good to go!*

Even if the next mirror would show the bags under the eyes, the dark veins, the bulges.

I don't know, honey, but I can tell you this: Since reading that affirmation, the mirrors in my house have occasionally laughed with me, not at me. Because it's true what they say—it's all about your attitude, your mental filter. For example, this declaration from the calendar: "I only accept beliefs that totally support me."

Why not?

Pick yourself up, honey. Let's give ourselves a break. Even the wicked queen who talked to the mirror, mirror on the wall got some good ratings before Snow White moved in, even if the queen did die at the end. *Never mind about that.*

Come on, honey. Let's be good to go. Here's waving right back at you.

Layer Three:
Coping

My yoga studio is on the bottom floor of the house. For years, students have parked their cars every which way on the street, marched down the stairs in tights and bare feet, and chanted staccato *ohms* led by the worst voice in the bunch, mine.

In between—on the upper floors and beyond—I write, patch up an old house, survive a kitchen abused by a bad cook, host family and friends and the occasional rude contractor or visiting mouse, and manage the stress of keeping things balanced like a shoulderstand, *sarvangasana,* the queen of all upside-down poses. Perched high on my shoulders, legs tall, chest open—I let shoulderstand scrub my brain, so my students think I know what I'm doing when I walk downstairs for that *ohm*.

Or maybe I do know. Maybe the one thing, the best thing, I learn from yoga is to practice keeping my head centered on my body no matter how late the story, no matter how deep the sludge to uncover an idea. After all, enlightenment—the ultimate goal of yoga and perhaps the greatest goal of all—promises emotional stability.

What? Me?

Some days, I trudge through the muck with the feeling of solid rubber boots—inviting, welcoming, celebrating another opportunity to practice what I preach, an undisturbed calmness of mind. *Really?* And some days, it's all quicksand.

Then I limp down to the studio and go upside down any feeble way I can so I don't crash into my wobbly two feet.

Home is where the mess is

Whenever I leave the house on a trip, I leave written instructions for Ray. Water the plants Friday, grab fruit at the farm market Saturday, pick up the dead branches blocking the front door, the ones you're stepping over. I try to be specific.

If it's not on the list, it doesn't exist.

After one trip, I entered a kitchen that smelled like a dozen females were having an intimate biological infection. That's the nicest way I can say it because this isn't a girls' lunch.

Ray's list didn't include every germ that could grow in a petri dish so I hold myself responsible. Though in my defense, I'd suggested if the fridge were opened now and again, it might be a good idea to throw out any sour milk, soggy greens, or oozing tomatoes that happened to crawl forward.

I meant to imply if an unusual rainbow of colors appeared behind those chilly metal doors—white foam, blue-black fuzz, green slime—please jump into action.

I should have written these exact words: "Bury your dead."

I have a great partner in the house so I shouldn't complain, besides it opens a whole can of worms, and I've yet to find any of those in the cheese drawer. I'm also committed to never dividing issues based on men versus women. I find it childish, overdone, boring, unfair, sexist, and generally untrue.

Though once in a while I wish these guys would open their eyes.

I've become even more vigilant about any organic festering because of a slew of E. coli outbreaks involving lettuce. I've been reminded not everything natural and plucky is good for us, even if it has lots of vitamins B and C along with gut-wrenching dysentery.

The E. coli issue sent me on a research rampage in which I discovered not everything tucked in the fridge is harmless, either. Lots of bacteria can grow in the icy climate of your home tundra, strange so-called psychrophiles lazing on the shelves, hiding behind the pineapple juice, making themselves comfy in your safe haven.

This cold-loving crud, maybe the weirdest poison on the planet, is also found in the glaciers of the Arctic and Antarctica. Heat-loving germs I understand; everything wants to spread out and proliferate when it's hot. But these cold suckers are way outside my comfort zone on every level.

I don't want to alarm you, but occasionally, you should get out the crampons and do a little exploration in your way-back forty to see if any glaciers are forming in there. Maybe you're even harboring a seal or a puffin.

Yet in all fairness, each time I leave the house, I notice the guy who must survive on Cheerios while I'm gone tries even harder not to let some silly oversight ruin our happy homecoming. And how could he remember Brussels sprouts, which he shuns, are not plant bulbs meant to be watered?

It wasn't on the list.

But to his credit, while I was away on a yoga retreat getting into the headspace I would need to enter the house, the refrigerator was filled up, even if it was covering up some pretty dicey items. In fact, while I was gone, we'd acquired six large onions and a dozen shiny Honeycrisps, because he'd forgotten he'd already bought them.

These new additions made me feel better. Some cultures believe onions have medicinal properties that could cure what ails you and maybe even give a creepy psychrophile a scary moment.

And certainly, I don't need to tell you about the health benefits of an apple a day. I've heard they even keep the puffins away.

Secrets of a rotten cook

I have a reputation for being a rotten cook. I know most people wouldn't brag, but I think it's a blessing. First, I can throw down a bag of iceberg and a boiled rutabaga and call it dinner, and second, I receive constant compliments from people who want to prove I'm wrong. "This instant oatmeal is just superb!" is the kind of praise I get all the time without hardly trying.

One of the reasons I like being a rotten cook is that it reminds me of my mother. After spending the whole day scrubbing, ironing, mopping, and sewing, she wanted to do something we'd actually appreciate. She let stews simmer until all the love she could pack in was fully absorbed, meaning everything was burnt to a crisp. I picked up lots of traits from her, but I can proudly say I got this one right. I can char a lentil loaf better than a five-alarm fire.

I also like being a rotten cook because it saves time. Great cooks are always dishing about their dishes and following cooking shows and collecting cookbooks and sharing recipes and tasting and adjusting and swooning.

I'm amazed at the amount of grating, dicing, and blanching that goes into the daily three squares.

In my own kitchen, I break out the machete. Vegetables get chopped like fireplace wood, thrown in a steamer, dumped in a bowl, and suffocated in soy sauce Monday to Friday, twice on Saturday, never on Sunday. On that day of recuperation, I'd rather take the soy sauce intravenously.

The only time the menu becomes a problem is when I have a dinner party. A bad cook and a dinner party go together like *beurre blanc* and salsa. But then I had a dream. A gourmet chef sat down next to me, pointed her finger, and gave me this big challenge: "Boost your ego, change your self-perception, and become more popular. Learn how to cook ten meals you can serve to a crowd."

Challenge accepted!

I started with my only success of the past, *Moosewood Cookbook's* to-die-for mushroom barley soup. I used to make it for birthdays, anniversaries, special holidays. Then everyone wanted the recipe for the one thing I could cook without a mass exodus.

But I needed to start with a bang. *Moosewood* holds up.

Happy and positive, I got to work on my second dish: Donna's savory eggplant and polenta party casserole, because I've learned it's pretty hard to screw up anything topped with tomato sauce. I ran to three stores before I found polenta and then chose an eggplant that appeared all shiny and plump. When I got home, I realized the polenta was the mashed kind, not the log, and the eggplant was rotten inside.

Did you notice in the old movie *Julie & Julia,* about Julia Childs and a food blogger named Julie, that Julie carts around one tiny bag of groceries for the whole dish she's about to make? And she never runs out for something she forgot. I need a caravan, a police escort, and a witch to get my ingredients home. Who has "eye of newt" just lying around?

Finally, I cut the new eggplant the wrong way and had to squish the slices together. The polenta broiled up to rawhide dog chewies. Is that the way it's supposed to look? Then I sautéed the mushrooms, boy, do they ever shrink. Okay, I'll add more. Then I shredded, shredded, shredded the mozzarella. And on top of everything I poured my one sure thing, tomato sauce. And voila! Red soup surrounding yellow hockey pucks laced with brown fungus and gooey yellow tentacles. Is the eggplant supposed to look like pieces of hanging flesh?

How hard is cooking? A male acquaintance asked me this, not realizing I was working on building my confidence and becoming more popular. His wife had burned their Sunday night chicken, and he trashed it. Literally.

I'm not sure what my dream chef would say about that overcooked chicken, but I know what my mother would say. His wife was probably making sure all the love she added, for him and him alone, was totally, utterly, achingly absorbed. Right down to every itsy-bitsy, teensy-weensy burned little bit.

Your mattress
or your life

Since we spend one-third of our lives sleeping, roughly twenty-five to thirty years in an average lifespan, it's a good idea to think about whether that part of our lives is working well. We can't always assume the Sandman is going to visit for eight glorious hours like when we were kids.

Instead, after the age of girlfriend sleepovers and college all-nighters, we need so-called sleep hygiene, those boring but necessary acts like tooth brushing that tell the brain it's time to say *Goodnight Moon* on a cozy, comfy mattress that floats us straight into oblivion.

Except if you've been snoozing on a hand-me-down used by your parents. *Caught!* Which brings up too many deep psychological issues to manage here so we'll simply focus on the practical.

Thus, my mattress adventure, an adult rite of passage, began. I invite you to join in my bounty of research and consider whether your own sleep surface—not your mate, friends, family, traffic, bad restaurants, nasty people, and the general miserable state of the world—is responsible for your daily grumblings about your sciatica, frozen shoulder, and foggy brain.

Let the education begin!

First you must determine if you're a back, side, or stomach sleeper. Some of us, as I learned the hard way, don't know until we stay up half the night watching the body flip and flail.

Apparently, back sleepers prefer medium firm mattresses, side sleepers softer, and belly sleepers firmest of all. Maybe.

Next step is to decide if you like foam, gel, latex, spring-and-coil with either pocketed or continuous coils, or a mashed-up hybrid that offers either fast or slow-acting foam on top of an innerspring. It may also contain fake smart gels to give you a natural, organic rest.

Some surfaces sleep hotter, some cooler. Some are bouncier, some so sinky you can hardly turn. Some have better edge support so you don't fall off, some so non-edgy it's tough to get out of bed without falling out. Some shoot you to an island with palm trees on a jet-propelled magic frame. I think one of my salespeople added that pitch as an extra incentive.

All mattress brands could work for all types of misshapen bodies depending on whether you customize with styles that are firm, luxury firm, palace firm, cushion firm, gentle firm, plush, luxury plush, or add an extra pillow top which could make a firm mattress less firm, which may be good for side and back sleepers but not so much for you belly downers, which by the way is quite an unhealthy way to sleep. Good luck trying to change now.

If you're part of a couple that sleeps together but on different parts of the anatomy, you may want to consider a dual-control airbed. And if you're a person who sleeps on all parts of the anatomy, constantly tossing and turning, you may want to consider surgery.

Don't even think about a waterbed. That's so frat party.

Experts say you need fifteen minutes to test a mattress. Bring along your favorite pillow and dress appropriately, no see-through nighties, because as you rest and roll, you may attract a crowd of curious onlookers out for a weekend jaunt.

Be prepared to spend most of your time craning your neck to gaze up at your salesperson as you sound thoughtful and intelligent about hot spots and air flow when all you want is a bedtime snack.

You could order a mattress online. This is quite popular and could be cheaper if you're the type who can buy something sight unseen and *presto*, it's yours for years to come. There are trial periods for these beds-in-a-box if you have the eventual energy to switcheroo. While you're testing, you can spend eight hours a night attempting to sleep while also examining your sleep, making you more likely to agree to sleep on anything.

To avoid that, I wrote this little piece while stretched out in full view at Macy's, debating if I had pressure points on my shoulders or my hips were dipping, both of which are bad. Or if my spine was truly straight, which is good. I've never had my natural curves examined by so many strangers in my life.

In the end—as confused as a sweet dream that turns into a sour nightmare—I still wondered what was too hard, too soft, too saggy, especially after a salesperson said, "Everybody is different. You and you alone must decide if the mattress is comfortable."

Funny, I thought the old one was, at least until I shopped for a new one. Now I have no idea how I've ever gotten a decent night's rest.

I hope this has been helpful. Goodnight, Macy's.

Reincarnate your lawn furniture

Our lawn furniture is descended from Bedouins. It's faded, dusty. Bits of sticks and foam poke out every which way like it's been carried across a desert. It smells like a camel.

Staring from inside the house, Ray and I watched families of squirrels coming and going through holes in the wicker, doorways to them.

"We promised to buy new stuff," I said. "Can't we just do it?"

"Do what?" he replied.

Money, they say, is the biggest thing couples fight about. We don't fight, we forget.

We forget about the lawn, too. We figure our lawn, after hundreds if not thousands or millions of reincarnations, should know by now how to maintain itself. Instead, it grows as if it wants to be a national park. My lawn has the biggest ego in the neighborhood.

My lawn furniture, on the other hand, has a small ego. It breaks, sags, and rusts, proving it's redundant to buy outdoor seating. That's why nature gave us trees, creating logs to sit on. That's why we have rocks.

Wrought iron is man's version of rock, so we thought it would last a lifetime, not rust away. Outdoor wicker is like branches, so we thought it would last a lifetime, too, not sprout sharp edges that poke the buttocks. Adirondack chairs made from rugged oak should also last a lifetime, not leave splinters that must be removed with garden shears.

Still, we'd rather scrutinize new furniture than fix old furniture, so we trudged to the patio emporium to suffer explanations about teak, cast aluminum, rattan, and shady umbrellas.

While we listened, we remembered this: Once you get the outdoor furniture home, it requires more work than the indoor furniture. You must seal it; you must store it. You must constantly check the weather. When it rains, you must manage the cushions so you can sit on them when the rain stops.

This means you need to put the cushions somewhere dry, but since they don't fit anywhere, you need to buy a special box. Then you need to find a place to put the box because you have a normal-sized yard, not a Rockefeller estate.

Add the exciting questions of mildew-resistant fabrics, side tables with sunken wine coolers, gliders that pacify unruly guests, fire-spewing coffee tables, deck heaters you use once a year but make you feel so European, and you have enough decisions for a lifetime.

Especially if your lifetime lasts longer than the so-called lifetime warranty on these goods—a mere seven years in some cases when you read the fine print, about the lifespan of a squirrel.

Burdened with enough detail to reincarnate as sales-people—*Your dream deck awaits!*—it was time to put our money where our mouths were. So we went out to eat.

Me: How many lifetimes do you think we'll have?

Ray: Before or after we eat these French fries?

Me: Can you eat French fries and still be reincarnated?

Ray: That depends on whether you put cheese on them.

Much as we tried, and though it was technically what we planned to discuss, we couldn't bring ourselves to talk about the lawn furniture we saw. A girl and a guy on a nice day sitting in a diner over potatoes chatting about cushions, it didn't seem right.

It's not that we hate spending money. We just hate spending money on the wrong things. If we got new stuff, the house would look very Martha Stewart on the outside and very shabby chic on the inside.

The squirrels would prefer it the other way around.

Perhaps, we realized, we were looking at this the wrong way.

Could it be our pathetic patio paraphernalia was perfect just the way it was?

Maybe the furniture wasn't all used up, maybe it had evolved into a more enlightened state? Maybe it had been reincarnated as an animal habitat?

I don't know, the squirrels running and jumping and playing, which is exactly what we should have been doing, looked pretty happy with things just the way they were.

The dog-in-law sleeps over

When I asked where Yasmine would sleep when we dog-sat her, my sister-in-law who lives in Germany looked at me in the same way the pug does: her eyes bugged out.

Then she shrugged her shoulders, spread her hands wide, and delivered the only answer that could keep this newly arrived animal from hellish nightmares: Yasmine sleeps *on* people.

Not *near* people. Not *next to* people. Not on the floor on a round tartan plaid cushion made for little pups. No. Yasmine sleeps *on top* of whoever is conveniently sprawled on a queen or preferably pillow-topped king-sized bed with a four-poster mahogany frame.

Since Ray and I already had a cat that sleeps on people, I wasn't surprised this animal enjoyed a warm, lumpy body. But I couldn't imagine how one old cat and one perky pug could sleep on top of each other, then sleep on top of us. We would be stacked like a layered vegetable torte, bound by eye drool, nose drip, and hair balls.

As the people on the bottom, we wouldn't sleep a wink. If the aging cat was the next layer, he'd heave his last breath when the dog came aboard. No matter which way the cards lay, it was dubious this group would stay in one uniform slab like cheese lasagna.

I looked at Helen and was instantly stifled. She had that far-away look in-laws get when they realize their relative has married someone less smart, attractive, or worthwhile than they are. If I didn't give in, this would be the new story they'd dredge up when hunched around a table whispering to each other. She and her German dog stared cold into my eyes.

The nerve of some species.

In a moment of forced compromise, Ray and I agreed we would sleep soundly in two separate rooms on two separate floors, each with a hefty weight on the chest.

May the best meowing, snorting pair win!

This is what I quickly learned about pugs: In addition to snorting, sniffing, and shedding, they snore worse than seven Rhodesian Ridgebacks. I don't mean an occasional wheeze or a consistent low hum; I mean violent fits and starts that make you think the canine will give birth to a construction site.

Once she cozied up to my face, I realized the night would be about one of two things: Either I'd listen to her oink and grunt for hours or push her like a tugboat to make her stop. She'd spend the night dreaming about German bratwurst, and I'd be ready to wrap the sausage around my neck.

Coping

Shocked that she, so far from home, was sleeping like a baby while I, in my own home, wasn't sleeping at all, I decided to simply stare at her. I hoped the energy of a dark presence would make her move away, just a little.

First her ears perked up. Then her ears went back. Then she moved, on her very own, and positioned herself a good few inches away with her head turned in the opposite direction. She was quiet.

I tried to figure her out.

She was a stalker but didn't want to be stalked. She was a sleeper but didn't let other people sleep. She was a comic. Pugs are known as the clowns of the dog world, and she could make you laugh just looking at her. But her sense of humor was fickle. She hated her dog halter, loved only designer water, and demanded enough apple chunks to keep the doctor away for a decade.

After a single burst of quiet, her motor revved again, and a night under the cat suddenly looked quite comfy. When I made Ray switch, I was accused of blowing things way out of proportion. He even suggested that I, as a vegetarian, secretly wanted to eat the meat Yasmine was dreaming about.

So I exaggerated. The way I see it, you need to throw a couple of pies, toot a couple of horns, and create a bit of a sideshow—with the help of a four-legged clown—to earn some serious paybacks from the in-laws.

Skeletons in the closet

Whenever I throw away something that's torn, scorned, long-ago worn, I have a philosophy. I walk it down to the giveaway pile in the basement, and I wait.

One day, two days, three.

A full seventy-two hours, a complete background check while the repository of my past, the unconscious, sorts through feelings and memories to reveal which dress, pants, shoes could haunt me for the rest of my natural-born life.

You don't want to mess with the unconscious.

If I'm not awakened in the middle of the night with panic for parting with a bustier, a flowered miniskirt, a pair of four-inch heels, they're good to go to another misguided Lolita.

But if my secret self is torn asunder, those seventy-two hours can be a torture of questions about whether I'll miss them, whether I'll feel guilty, whether I'll need them to satisfy some primitive urge, and if I do, whether I'll be able to replace them down to every stain and stitch.

Letting go is so much easier when it's someone else's junk.

For example, when my sister Shara moved to Florida, she couldn't even part with her honey, and I'm not talking about her husband. I'm talking Trader Joe's raw honey crystallized in a jar.

I promised to give it a good home.

I slogged through every decision with her: Keep, give away, donate, trash, repurpose, beg, plead. We weighed the keepsake quality of hair oil, get well cards, dirty baseball caps, bent silverware, dying plants, photos of people she didn't know. Every little thing collected in her big house with three kids over twenty years.

Even using the three-day rule, she knew a Day Four emergency was a distinct possibility.

The rusted fry pan? I know it's seen better days, she said, *but ...*

The frog vase? I know it's ugly, *but ...*

The muddy door mat? The Halloween vampire? *But, but, but ...*

I came home peeved. "How about my junk?" I yelled to the basement as I went down to check the growing pile. "Does she think she's the only one trapped by her trash? Take mine, *please.*"

My unconscious sighed *but, but, but ...*

Remember how you felt in that dress? Sophisticated. Remember what you served on those dishes? Fancy. Remember the rooms that held that painting? Cozy. If I give away the memorabilia, will the memories remain?

I opened boxes stored on a high shelf to peer at mysteries inside, convinced if I collect less now, I'll suffer less later. Maybe one day I could even move without an army.

I came across a silver box that said "La Canadienne, Black, Waterproof." Empty.

Of course, it once held my favorite sleek, walkable boots. They never sit out a season, always have a sacred place on the floor of my closet.

But the silver box? I mean really.

I added it to the junk pile, and I waited. One day, two days, three. Torture.

"Surely, it's a perfectly good box," I heard a nagging voice say. *"Nice and sturdy, and what harm does it do? And what if you lose the shoes someday, could you find them again without the details on that dusty lid. They were likely discontinued last century, but you never really know."*

The voice warned: *"This is wasteful, you are ungrateful, you will be remorseful. Put it back on the shelf where it belongs."*

I called my sister and told her I share her sickness, maybe it's genetic. Every bracket and bracelet, every picture and pot somehow has meaning.

But it's not our fault.

Our houses may be full, but the unconscious, the original hoarder extraordinaire, always seems to have room for one more thing. Maybe that dusty silver box will give it a little more space for storage.

I cleaned the cat

With twenty relatives coming for the Thanksgiving holiday, the house seemed all wrong, especially the faux maple leaves bought to decorate the table so it would scream FESTIVE!

My confidence wavering, I decided to put the blame on the first victim I found: the cat.

If only his tongue and fur, like the guests coming to dinner, would connect. If only he would wash himself, the rest of the holiday would take care of itself.

The stuffing would be moist, the cauliflower would get eaten, and Ray's family and mine would avoid testy topics: Politics, global warming, health care, UFOs, big business, genetically modified food, and the appropriateness of eating Chinese eggrolls and Japanese sushi for American appetizers. Did the Pilgrims eat that?

But the seventeen-year-old feline Yoda, both oily as salmon and wrinkly as his namesake, the wizened Jedi from "Star Wars," washed no more.

The Jedi might advise: Clean not cat. Roast not turkey. Reinvent Mayflower no. Too much work Thanksgiving is.

Where's a Jedi master when you need him?

After cleaning the cabinets, the refrigerator, the couches, the rugs, the floors, the wine glasses, and my mother's old silver, I bought a new coffeepot, casserole dishes, tablecloth, ice bucket, sofa pillows, and sheets and blankets for the guests who would stay the weekend. I found new family photos to put in old frames, rearranged the plants, artwork, and candles. Unfortunately, without the benefit of Jedi wisdom, I then turned my attention to the cat.

Panicked after the dishwasher broke, I fixed my steely eyes on Yoda.

Was it true he'd never had a bath? He was old, his back legs barely worked, his fur flaked off if you blew on him, and he stumbled around between sleeping twenty-three hours a day and drinking a vat of water for his aging kidneys.

"If the cat lives through Thanksgiving," I pronounced, "the cat will be clean."

As with any hostage, this fated feline knew his days were numbered. When Ray and I began whispering in the kitchen, he lasered a cold, green stare, bared his still sharp teeth, ejected his still sharp claws, then turned on his sagging gray tabby legs and careened across the tile floor in search of cover.

Cat leave. Basement you run. Bad time coming it is. Hide you must.

The plan went this way: we would lure him to the upstairs bathroom with a handful of his beloved Quaker Rice Puffs, slowly caress him, lovingly drip soap on his fragile body, then aggressively pour buckets of water on the drowned rat until he completely flipped out.

We dressed in riot gear, thinking of the Pilgrims with barely a body part showing, and Jedi foe Darth Vader, with no face showing at all. We put on ski pants, rain jackets, face masks, gloves, bubble wrap. I took out the hydrogen peroxide, antibiotic ointment, Band-Aids, Valium, defibrillator, and Hoover Wet Dry Vac. The last time we washed a cat, long before Yoda, it was a fight that ended with both of us pressed against the walls, both of us equally soaked, both of us with hair standing on end, droplets of blood everywhere.

This holiday tale ended better. I learned cleaning an old cat is like a big family dinner. At first, there's a lot of nervousness, but eventually everyone calms down and accepts who they can't sit next to, what favorite foods are missing, and who they wish they could punch. Yoda accepted his fate for a good five minutes and when we freed him from the porcelain tub, he made a swift retreat to his special corner, rolled up in a ball, and tried to recover from his Thanksgiving ordeal. He even, shockingly, licked his imagined wounds.

Come to think of it, that's what a lot of people do when the long holiday weekend is over.

The pink bathroom

I have a pink bathroom. The kind of pink only girls under five would like. Over the years, I've grown fond of it. Not because of the color, but because it's the one room in the house people get enthusiastic about. Whenever I mention the pink bathroom, everyone wholeheartedly agrees it must be renovated immediately.

I thought so, too, but then one thing led to another, and what I originally said I couldn't live with for ten minutes, I lived with for ten years. Partly because most of the time I'm completely confused about what's in or what's out as far as home fashion is concerned.

Something that might appear "so 1950s" to one person, which is bad, is "retro" to another, which is good. Something that implies to one person that you live in a barn, which is bad, might be rustic to another, which is good. And something that looks Zen to one person, which is good, could look cold and sparse to another, which is bad.

How do designers have the vaguest idea what styles to develop when a fifteen-hundred-dollar faucet that could blow a whole renovation budget looks like a centerpiece of Greco-Roman splendor to one person and an outdated relic of feminist repression to another? All I know is when I started shopping with a redo in mind—under threat from those who refused to visit the pink throne—I was flush with confusion about what I like, what I hate, and what I don't care a pink pansy about.

Truth is, I've hardly remodeled since outhouses came indoors. I spend most of my time figuring out how to get out of the house, not stay in it. Why make it more attractive so instead of packing a bag, I want to flop on a sofa with a good book while the world passes me by? *Hmmm ...* doesn't sound so bad, does it?

So to catch up with the rest of you, I decided to give it a go. Day in and day out, I started learning the fine nuances of bathroom language: the differences between dual versus gravity flush, overhead halogens versus incandescent sconces, single lever versus two-handled shower control. Everywhere I went I saw people poring over books and colors and materials and matching up squares of tile with squares of wood with squares of paint and then standing back and doubting and swapping and standing back again while salespeople weaved in and out figuring out how to keep their mouths shut except for, "Everything looks lovely, just lovely, what a great palette."

"Just buy what you like" is one of the more bizarre pieces of advice you get. Whenever I hear it, I engage in a seesaw battle. One part of me detests matchy-matchy, another respects order and symmetry. One part of me wants to follow the rule of "it's just not done," another wants to install a fish-inspired hot tub smack in the middle of the room.

All of which got me thinking about an unrenovated barn, not a renovated one, where all you worry about is straw. But how many kinds of straw do they make these days, and how soft or rough or perhaps hand-dried in the Colorado sun or tinted in timeless terrestrial tans? And how about hinges in antique brass or brushed chrome to secure the old doors, and shall we finish them in honey or bronze or ginger with espresso glaze?

Or maybe even pink, which now and again returns to fashion. Which brings me back to square one and my original theory on renovation. It's best considered with one eye closed and the other on a plain black suitcase, single handled and double wheeled, with as many stains as possible. No additional glaze required.

Let's admit,
let's regift

Q: What do these three things have in common? A Vladimir Putin bobble head, a frog ashtray, and Dionysus, the God of wine, entombed on a mirror frame, his voracious eyes bugged, his mouth dripping.

A: Nobody wants them.

I know this because when someone—*anyone*—visits, I beg them to take them out of my house. Old gifts, bad gifts. I get on my knees, I plead.

But thanks to a pact proposed in a park by my blood-sharing relatives, this could someday end. During a walk to burn off a holiday brunch, we suggested it was time to stop the annual ritual of buying people we dearly love presents they dearly hate.

Never again did we wish to join the yearly lineup of overburdened souls returning their saddest rejects if they have receipts. Never again did we want the flotsam and jetsam to go to that dark place in every home where ties, socks, mugs, fake snakes from Tibet carried across oceans by euphoric relatives, lie in wait.

The idea took root when one sister gave my nephew Josh a basket of used toys for his toddler. "I'll wrap them for Christmas," he responded, knowing they'd be loved briefly then shoved to the side like peas on a plate. Some family members were slightly horrified, others laughed, others kept their wise mouths shut.

Then a light went off. This made sense. All of us had old stuff, good stuff, useful stuff, even brand-new stuff we couldn't stand looking at another minute. Why not regift it all, maybe to the very people who gave it to us?

One brother-in-law took the legal view: "The thing is yours, it's part of your property, and you're giving a part of your property away. What's wrong with that?"

One sister built on the climate change crisis: "Let's recycle, renew, repurpose." Another thought of frugal home renovation: "Refresh, redesign, redo."

Then there was the stress-reduction rationale: "If we don't worry about the perfect gift, we'll be investing in the family's health." And the cathartic clear-the-air idea: "Let's show each other what we really thought of the junk they bought us."

And finally, we launched the new family rallying cry: "Let's admit, let's regift," which we chanted over and over as we marched.

Through twists and turns in the park, we hatched the plan. The next year, we would bring whatever we thought was good enough, clean enough, or weird enough, and place it on the family holiday table, a banquet of rejected goods.

With glee, we would grab and switch, snatch and trade, until whatever was left—the grossest of the gross—would be thrown in a bin and donated, if anyone would have them.

A smart, honest, cheap, and potentially riotous family tradition was born, and we did it together. How cool were we! We turned to each other, in a circle, our hands outstretched to shake on it.

Or at least some of us did.

There were skeptics, like the younger folks, not sure they'd enjoy giving up the latest and greatest for the oldest and lamest. But some adults were also holding back.

A holiday without new stuff? A holiday with bad stuff? Would that really be a holiday or an ugly day?

When it came right down to it, despite all our chants and chutzpah, the concept worked better in the woods than it did in the parking lot as we got ready to leave. We got in our cars; the deal had not been sealed. Yet.

Yes, when it came right down to it, it seemed a lot of us still wanted new junk, especially junk thoughtfully bought *specifically* for cherished, adored us.

What are you doing with that zucchini?

Every now and then, panting like an anxious dog, Ray storms into the house and blows a whistle on privacy invasion in the most unlikely places: the coffee shop, the gas station, Target. It sounds like this:

Ray: Do you know what the cashier at Whole Foods had the guts to ask?

Me: My corn ears are open.

Ray (hyperventilating): What are you planning to do with that cabbage?

To me this seemed like a small thing, even a friendly, warm, community thing. To him, it's information spies would carry to Russia.

Ray: Phone calls, texts, emails, fine. I can't do a thing about them. But I draw the line on a total stranger asking me a probing question about my vegetables.

He was also stalked carrying his Starbucks into Nordstrom.

Stylish Saleswoman: What do you have in that cup?

Ray: Ummm ... coffee.

S.S.: Oh, I prefer latte or cappuccino. I like my coffee strong.

Ray: You should go to Europe; they like strong coffee there.

S.S.: Oh, I would never go to Europe. I hear they're fashionable over there and I'm not fashionable. (She was wearing a miniskirt and over-the-knee boots.) I think I'll go to Japan.

Ray: Uhhh … *what?*

I had to admit this was suspicious, maybe some obscure international spy code. Who doesn't know Japan is ultra-chic? Before I knew it, I was noticing things, too.

Pedicurist: Got any plans for the weekend?

Me: Yes.

Was something more required? Or could I relax for one hour in my interrogation chair?

The whole thing suddenly went from suspicious to paranoid.

Barnes & Noble Salesperson to Ray: *Lawrence in Arabia* by Scott Anderson? Nice book choice.

He thought his mind was being mined. He feared if he had any sense, he should grab his book and cold coffee and make a getaway until his tracks ran cold.

The issue was raised at a dinner party. Ray wondered if other people wanted to buy lotion without being asked where they itched.

One guest mewed it was all about making the world a kinder, gentler place, brushing away the hardness of us against them. Another said the questions and answers helped newbie employees, like the young ones at the market who barely know a Pink Lady apple from a Granny Smith.

Ray (not buying it): Today it's cabbage. Tomorrow it's, "What are you going to do with that zucchini?"

After a pregnant pause, we had to admit he had a point.

Ray (turning in my direction): Go buy the weirdest vegetable at Whole Foods and see what happens. I'm telling you, it's some underground training manual they're working with over there. You can't get out the door without handing over your famous family recipes.

Let the inquisition begin.

I drove to the market and bought my weekly stash, adding a big bold jicama. Or was it a turnip? A giant white radish? A plump and hard-shelled pear from the scorched earth of a desperate country? I was anticipating all kinds of curious inquiries as I shimmied toward a promising lane with a secret agent cashier, a seemingly perky girl-next-door type with a fresh-as-a-cucumber look, ready to spy on me.

Secret Agent: I see you buy a lot of vegetables. You must be very healthy. And if you don't mind me saying, you sure do look it!

Me: Uhhh ... Got any plans for the weekend?

Starving
perfectionists eat

I come from a family of starving perfectionists. Among us there are two medical degrees, one law degree, one engineering degree, one veterinarian, master's degrees in business and counseling, a couple of writers, decades of training in organizational change, years of experience in teaching, design, public relations, and office management, a dedicated yogi, a magician, and a number of clearly talented children destined to become great humanitarians.

Despite all this knowledge, not one of us can put together an all-American meal. We can save the desperately ill, argue complicated points of law, debate the per capita income of Saudi Arabia, conduct gripping interviews, and connect directly with the spirit world, but we can't keep ourselves gorged on a special occasion.

It's not because we're ignorant of the ingredients required, or the nutritional values of dairy fat versus olive oil, for example, or the best way to steam a fish. Oh no, we not only read the book, we could have written it. It's because no food anywhere is ever perfectly fresh, impeccably seasoned, served at the exact right temperature, and paired with the ideal accompaniment. We have too many gourmet cookbooks and not enough gourmet cooks. Too many hands in the nutrition books and not enough in the nonstick pots. We're dripping with knowledge and dry as a bone in juicy sauces. We're swimming in great ideas, but the gravy boat is empty.

Before a special meal, my hungry sisters, Caryl and Shara, choose recipes. Then they send those recipes certified mail to all designated contributors to the feast. Do not, under any circumstances, create your own similar dish. It must be organic, red-skinned potatoes grown in the hills of Nebraska and tossed with crushed Hawaiian macadamia nuts and fresh basil, or it must be no dish at all. Preferably, the basil is shipped overnight in sealed banana leaves.

If you use something else, like basil in rice paper, you will be glared at in the kitchen where everyone ends up anyway because we must dust just a dash more cinnamon on the apple envelopes, brown the top layer of the cauliflower casserole to achieve a dusky shade of taupe, and sauté the wild Coho salmon until the middle inner flesh is exactly as flaky as the outside.

Everyone is fainting, but no one is eating.

Meantime, in the flurry of perfection, no one has remembered three additional dishes have been stored in a downstairs refrigerator. The cranberries with chestnuts are never served, the exotic fig loaf is never cut, and the simple broccoli with nothing added—just to clear the pallet—is never steamed.

Coping

The two family members with hypoglycemia get challenged at some point. We intravenously inject them with an emergency loaf of Stroehmann's, then use this opportunity to discuss the value of twelve-grain bread versus mushy white, while the corn soufflé is popping and the baby asparagus are wailing.

If any of the food does make it to the table, the room is hushed and somber as the first bite is taken. Then all cutlery stops. The hypoglycemics pause mid-fork, the children who've been pacified with Skittles and M&Ms are bouncing off their seats, and the criticism begins. The spices are way too overpowering in one dish, another is way overcooked so all the vitamins have leached out, still another is so burnt it's like pumping ash directly into the lungs. Even the hypoglycemics suddenly become full and everyone is tearing into the Stroehmann's just to say a meal has been eaten.

Then we rush to the fridge and pull out a chocolate mousse or a gallon of vanilla. Don't we deserve it? We tried so hard. Then we lovingly kiss and hug as we talk of the next ideal feast already on our tongues while the dog gorges on leftovers.

We have not sunk below our ideals. And thanks to a little Häagen-Dazs, another family meal has ended in perfection.

Layer Four:
Straying

T he first time I knew travel was for me, though my family never went beyond the New Jersey shore, was when I stood on Blue Jay Way in Los Angeles at twenty, on a summer trip with my equally gaga girlfriends. The lights, the view, the illegal intoxicants—I was swept away.

Writing is like that, too. You watch, listen, investigate, running your experiences through an internal scanner, putting pieces together into uncharted terrain that makes you feel curious, inspired, alive, maybe a tiny bit scared.

Yoga also sweeps you away from your tried but maybe no-longer-true cushy comfort. It demands you unclutter your mind and ready your body for unexplored territory.

You never know when the next adventure will occur. Not an encounter with an unsavory character perhaps, but an encounter with a shady part of yourself you've yet to befriend.

For example, you don't tackle your first *pincha mayurasana*—an upside-down pose that balances on the elbows—without some idea of where to put your arms and legs. You must be conscious of what's happening everywhere at once, so you can venture onward without getting yourself into too much trouble. In theory.

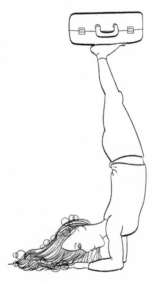

You stand facing a wall, put your forearms down on the ground, lift your hips high in the air, throw your legs up one at a time, you balance. Your perspective—*Help! Where are my feet?*—has changed. That scary yet alive thing that builds confidence, self-trust, courage.

And neither yoga nor writing asks that you leave your house on a risky, stressful, possibly life-threatening escapade.

Must remember next time.

Pack for me

I f you're a woman, and you go somewhere, anywhere, packing may be the worst part of the journey. We can outwit dangerous border patrols with a gut-wrenching story or navigate bizarre foreign rules with a *s'il vous plait* on bended knees, but we can't figure out which pants go for two solid weeks without chafing, pinching, stretching, fading, sticking, wrinkling, itching, staining, or making us look fat, old, dumpy, dull, out of style, out of season, or under serious threat of showing underwear.

In under ten minutes, Ray lays crisply folded T-shirts end to end in his tiny suitcase and places one, maybe two pairs of pants on top and then applies sunscreen and breaks out a magazine. Meantime, I tear open storage cabinets, upend shoe boxes, and try on lavish gowns I haven't worn since prom days to be sure I've probed all possibilities. He even keeps lists from past vacations so he can grab the same pants and shirts for a trip five years later. He stares as I sit on my suitcase to mask its bulging contents. Fancy baubles slip out beneath my body.

"How do you know we won't be invited to a ball?" I scream. "How do we ever really know?"

We don't know and that's the problem. Those who claim they know risk being prepared for nothing but miniature golf. I, however, am prepared for road work, a black-tie affair, and bowling. Once when I packed light, I ended up in a four-day monsoon with only beachwear. Another time my blue jeans were stolen from a clothesline, and I had to look cool, to my twenty-something horror, in khakis.

It's well known that flight attendants are the world's packing-light experts. That's the one reason I've wanted to be one. They make one item do the work of eleven and find that perfect black suit that goes everywhere. Sure, Birmingham to Brussels, but to Patagonia? To the Pushkar Camel Fair in India? What if my flight is diverted to Madagascar, or I must forge continents in a global warming exodus?

I have one female relative who breaks the mold. She packs so light she carries everything in a coin purse. I won't say her clothes look slept-in because she might be reading this, and she'll know I'm talking about her. She thinks she's the only woman on earth who packs like a man. I didn't say she looks like a man. Don't put words in my mouth.

I have a relative at the other extreme, too. She packed seventeen pairs of shoes for three days in Florida, hiding them inside her pocketbook, her trench coat, her blow-up plane pillow. On the surface these two relatives seem as different as first class and coach, but I see them as the same.

One can't pack to save her life, and the other can't save her life with what she's packed. One carries smelling salts, shoe stretchers, a hot steam vaporizer, long satin gloves. When she gets where she's going, she could walk the red carpet, breathing easily and in comfortable shoes, and be quickly revived if she faints from the pressure. The other carries the clothes on her back plus microwave popcorn. When she gets where she's going, all she can do is watch movies in the hotel.

In lieu of a wise woman to look up to, I'm going with this: the vaporizer stays but the satin gloves come because they dress up any outfit. Beyond that, if I get the chance, I'm switching my carry-on with the black look-alike of a similarly sized flight attendant who happens to bump into me in an airport ladies' room, leaving her bag unattended.

With security being what it is, she should be ashamed of herself for letting it out of her sight for a second. And with travel being what it is, who could blame me for nabbing such a perfectly packed treasure.

Is your "inner captain" stuck in lingerie?

Remember that riddle where a kid is rushed to the emergency room after being in a car accident with his father, and when the kid reaches the hospital, the surgeon says, "Oh my gosh, my son?"

How could the father be in two places at once?

Because, you sexist, the surgeon was his mother.

Shockingly, when I came face-to-face with my first female jet pilot, that sexist idiot was me.

The woman who held my life in her hands was a lanky blonde dressed in a male captain's suit with unflattering short sleeves that barely revealed her well-cut arms. This made me fear girls could not be trusted in the cockpit.

I turned to Ray and said, "We're late taking off. Do you think she was primping?"

"Sexist," he shot.

The pilot, her disembodied voice coming over the loud-speaker, admitted we were way behind schedule: "We were delayed coming in last night because of the weather, so the crew didn't get much sleep."

"Not much sleep?" I mumbled, squinting my eyes and pursing my lips. "I wonder if she was up all night chatting with her friends?"

"So sexist, I can't believe it," Ray groaned. "Now, shush."

"I also got up at 3 a.m. to make this flight," I blurted, "but you don't see me donning a captain's suit, slipping into a cockpit, and flying an Airbus 319. Maybe she's in the middle of a dream about a real McCoy pilot."

"If you don't shut up, I'll turn you in as a sexist terrorist," Ray barked, craning his head left and right, hoping to catch another glimpse of our leggy leader.

I was primed for this lesson in humility. The previous weeks had seen lots of vitriol thrown at a conservative news commentator who supposedly refused to fly with a black woman pilot. A heinous action, we all thought, then we learned we were duped. It apparently never happened.

But this was happening, for real. The main door of the airplane was closed, preparations for takeoff were underway, and I was stuck in my seat, a combination of charmed and chagrined. There was nowhere to go but up. I stared at the cockpit door, pondering my reaction.

Though I'm bullish on equality, breaking the glass ceiling, and supporting women—*My God! Supporting women everywhere!*—still I wondered what was happening behind the barrier. Secretly, I wondered if she was being manly in there, maybe scratching her chest and taking a swig of strong coffee to get her chutzpah going.

Or was she meditating, praying for good luck as she made a mental checklist of lingerie to buy when she landed.

"Maybe she needs a massage," I said to Ray and smirked. "Wanna go ask?"

"Stop kidding around," he hissed, "and admit you're jealous."

Fine, I admit it. Women who are capable in all things technical and mechanical make me green with envy, more than a dozen skinny models ever could. I fit a stereotype about women that's appallingly lame: I'm a mental midget when it comes to getting things to work.

Give me a bottle of shampoo and I'll spend an hour trying to get the dispenser to pop up. Give me a map and I'll turn it upside down then call a cop for help. Give me an error message on my computer and I'll scream like the whole thing blew up and took the house with it.

With women being a tiny 1 percent of airline captains in the world, I was so impressed she could fly this thing I couldn't quite understand it. I wanted to climb into the cockpit, pick her brain, and shake her hand. Or give her a hug. She probably needed one if forced to fly to boring Paris or Rome over and over again. I decided right then and there I wanted to find my inner captain, too. I wanted to believe I could carry the weight of a jet with 150 passengers on my own girl shoulders, or at least get my carry-on out of the overhead without it crashing to the ground.

And maybe, with her as my role model, I could. Although we took off an hour late, we arrived twenty minutes early. My pilot juggled the schedule as only a woman can (stereotype), obviously knowing that arriving on time is unexpected for a woman (stereotype). Nothing gives a female more confidence than proving old myths are just that.

As a woman and a zero in all things that fly, drive, beep, squawk, and sputter around, I stand accused of being jealous, yet at the same time inspired. Next time, I swear, I'll get the overhead light to pop on without calling a flight attendant for help.

Sleep like an animal

T he thing I admire most about animals is how well they sleep. They can sleep on a cliff or underwater. They can sleep piled on top of each other or balanced on one leg. They can sleep with food hanging out of their mouths and sand and flies encrusting their bodies.

I was reminded of this on a trip to the Galapagos Islands. In the middle of everything but in the middle of nowhere, with no blankets or hot tea or nature sounds spilling out of earbuds, the sea lion, for example, can sleep. Here in the human world, we need rituals like taking a hot bath or supportive yoga poses or watching something soothing like the nightly news.

In the animal world, even making the bed is wasted time for the big payoff: dead-to-the-world sleep. You can leap over the catatonic sea lion, entertain him with the frantic mating dance of the famous Galapagos blue-footed booby, and yell "Plankton, lots and lots of plankton," and that slimy sand-caked sausage would only swat the couple of flies eating out its eyeballs.

They don't care if the air conditioner is clangy, the room is muggy, or the neighbor's TV is blasting. Give the sea lion an inch and he'll figure out how to sleep in it without caring a flying fish if the pillows are puffed.

And a flying fish is a pretty special meal.

When you go to the Galapagos, the mating behavior of the naked animals may be the thing you want to see, if you're a guy. But there's not a woman on the planet who would trade knowledge of a good night's sleep for a bizarre sex routine. I wanted to see the animals up close and personal for a reason less perverted but equally voyeuristic: to pick up sleep pointers, because it could take a village to work this thing out.

In this case, the ingredients were a village of exotic species plus insects, rocks, mud, caves, and absolutely—if my sampling of this animal world was right—no memory foam at all.

You may think there's no need to travel far and wide to imitate animal behavior. You can do it right at home with the family cat, one of those eighteen-hour-a-day sleepers that takes every opportunity to recover from living.

But watching the cat can be dangerous. To him, we're predators. You can stare all day at the Galapagos animals because they don't have predators. Not so with Fluffy. You could give him nothing but food and affection, yet he'd believe you were stalking him. I've had tracks on my arms, legs, cheeks to prove it.

But on those distant islands, the sea lion swims with me, which makes me happy. And the big land tortoise walks in my direction, which makes me happy. And the spooky iguana sits and stares at me, which makes me happy. In every case I'm temporarily free from rejection.

This is the main reason, of course, we can't sleep. All the rejection, projection, and fear that one day, no matter how good and perfect we are, we will find ourselves washed up on some distant prehistoric shore.

The sea lion doesn't know his day will come. Or the tortoise. Or the brown bat that sleeps a whopping twenty hours a day.

Which brings us to the first big secret I learned on those craggy volcanic islands.

To sleep like there's no tomorrow or yesterday or even today, you must sleep like there's nothing but fish—schools and schools of fish, growing, spreading, jumping, glowing—more and more fish from now until the end of time.

To sleep like an animal, you must think like an animal. Or not think like one.

Meaning, stop thinking about anything but your kind of fish, fried or broiled. Then load up whenever you can, and everything else should fall into place just fine. Roll in the mud or the sand or the sea, do not under any circumstances clean yourself unless you have a wedding. Drop wherever you fall, be willing to sleep the sleep of sloths no matter what you miss, and bottom line: if the sun doesn't shine tomorrow morning, so long as you're sound asleep, who gives a flying fish.

I was confused. What part did I play in the movie going on in my head? Was I the hustler in the muscle shirt or the hussy in the miniskirt?

Game One: It looked so neat (an uncool word) when the cue ball bounced like a Ping-Pong ball, one of the six-year-olds in the crowd ran over and asked if he could play, too. We played. We bounced. His parents thanked me for being a great babysitter.

Game Two: After correcting my front hand, back grip, elbow angle, stance, tip position, follow through, and hairstyle—"Spike it up, you need more attitude"—Ray played a very mean game. He quickly sank every ball, forcing me to show sickening awe. In cool response, I wrapped the cue stick behind my back for a trick shot. The stick flailed up; it flailed down. I looked like I was playing a violin concerto.

Game Three: I recruited another couple, hoping to divert the focus of the growing crowd attracted to my game. Or maybe the hangers-on were just trying to steal the table. The new woman also shot the so-called girl way but with better luck. I used the open grip, ready to decimate the nine ball then set up and sink the four. All eyes glared as the cue ball limped across the table like a disembodied organ and lay there pleading for help.

I surrendered my stick.

"What happens in Maine stays in Maine," I announced to no one in particular, as I grabbed my coat and turned toward the door. For some cool reason—maybe my spiked-up hair, maybe the far away stars watching from on high—everyone applauded.

The movie faded to black ...

*Nemo's did one day catch fire and burn down. I guess it wasn't quite "cool" enough.

Kick the bucket list

H ang glide over the Rockies? Start the great American novel? Make apple pie from scratch?

Organize your family photos? *Fuhgeddaboudit!* Otherwise, no time like the present to tackle the bucket list. But the dream is just a dream, and the pie is from a box if you don't have apples and don't go into the kitchen.

So, in the spirit of bringing Mohammed to the mountain, I boarded a boat on the west coast of Iceland praying for a lucky break to see the biggest creature on earth, the largest animal that's ever lived, twice the size of measly T. rex, the kingliest, the most gigantic, the most behemoth of the behemoths—and how often can you use the word behemoth?—the sleek, elusive, one-hundred-foot, two-hundred-ton blue whale in the frigid waters near the Arctic Circle. Cold is its thing with all that warm blubber, and hopefully it would have some friends and relatives nearby.

The more behemoths the better. Once you say the word, you can't stop tickling your fancy of possibility. This isn't your average Big Mac or Big Gulp.

If Big Blue is not on your bucket list, at least it should be on your list of bodyguards.

The tongue of the blue whale can weigh as much as an elephant. Their hearts can be the size of a car. You could park your SUV right in its mouth and pay nothing but some crusty krill the size of a pinky finger, because these guys are crazy for tiny. Go figure.

So, with big on my brain and tiny on theirs, a bit of seasickness medication in my belly, and the bucket list close to kicking the bucket, time's a wastin', I donned a whale-sized bright blue jumpsuit and shuffled onboard looking like my underwater idol.

I wouldn't do this for any other mammal.

As I waited with krill-full breath, I thought:

What is the bucket list, anyway, but a bunch of apple pies in the sky, self-delusional musings, imaginary "if onlys?" Do we ever think we'll get through it all, and will we forgive ourselves if we don't? At some point, don't we realize we can't go everywhere and do everything that life has to offer?

It's both a relief and a bummer.

What, then, stays on the list? Maybe the dreams we want badly enough, more achingly bad than the rest, and could actually make happen. Unless we think we're too old or too nervous or too busy or too dumb.

How do we light a fire under the blubber?

Fortunately, as I meditated on questions larger than the largest creature spanning the oceans, Big Blue was not contemplating its own salad-plate-sized navel, but swimming in my general direction.

Success! And it even brought friends and family!

We saw four blue whales that day, though I can't figure how the guides knew it wasn't the same one over and over. We watched their sleek bodies slip in and out of the waves, their flapping flukes rise and dip, their majestic sprays rain down upon the deep.

Not enough, in my naïve opinion, to know if it was Sue or Bill. But one apparent Sue had a baby Suzie with her, which thrilled us all to no end.

I've never made a quiche from scratch, though I've always wanted to. Or taken a painting class. Or learned French like a real Frenchwoman. Or gone to bed whenever I damn well please for days on end, not caring one whit about being off kilter with the whole wide world.

Not everything on the list requires a plane flight, seasick meds, and a lot of luck.

Time to move more blubber?

Avoid these people

I'm amazed how many people I know, yet never see, in my busy metropolis. Some even live right around the corner. Decades could go by.

Even people I used to be in love with. One day it was fair weather and the next, it was like a hurricane blew through and they disappeared in the debris.

Such can be the anonymous big cities we live in.

Not so on the tiny island of St. John, as I was reminded on a winter beach escape. It's the kind of place where the sun shines on every resident like a police interrogation spotlight at 2 a.m.

Staying anonymous on St. John is like keeping your rum and coke cold in eighty-five-degree weather.

While I held onto my melting drinks, day after day I learned about Lil, Bob, Tina, Dawn, Jeanne, Jane, Ralph, and Suzanne. Since you may never meet any of them and I've messed with their names, I thought I'd share some of the tasty tidbits that kept showing up as common as conch fritters.

Lil was voracious where gossip was concerned, sort of like the predatory lionfish infesting the Caribbean reefs. She got the whole ball rolling.

Lil: Under no circumstances should you go to Dawn's Café.

Me: What's wrong with Dawn?

Lil: She's a pushy mainlander. We need to send her back to the frigid States where she belongs.

Knowing we were, well, city people ourselves, for the rest of the trip we avoided Lil. And of course, we avoided Dawn.

Then there was Bob, the most helpful guy, until we heard from Jeanne he raced hermit crabs for a living, those red crawly things always fighting for a bigger shell. Since I collect shells, we avoided Bob, afraid he'd turn my collection into a homeless shelter.

Jeanne, meanwhile, disclosed she'd had such a heap of trouble in her old life, all she could do in her new one was snorkel alone, venting her frustration on those invasive lionfish, then hole up in her boat.

Avoid her, we figured, because we were invading her space just by sharing her deep blue sea.

Tina from the jewelry shop was a gem, we thought. Then Ralph from the burger joint, who announced he was "recovering," said shun Tina like a sea urchin. Something about her being a raging alcoholic—it took one to know one—who sues everyone because she "accidentally" slips and falls.

Ralph: Beware of Tina.

In no time at all, I started feeling I knew the locals down there better than the ones at home. In my own town, I've gone to the same Farmer's Market for years. I see the same sellers, visit the same stalls, collide with the same neighbors, but honestly, I don't know who hits the bottle or who hits his wife.

On St. John, within a week, I knew who called the cops to have the beer store shut down, who ran the landmark diner into the ground, who was a gang member.

Jane from the smoothie stand, for example, was a thief. Seems she stole her land from the government but had lived there so long no one knew how to get rid of her. Suzanne, meantime, was a sweet young thing who announced she had seizures and needed her trusty service dog, Pedro, nearby. We later saw her chain smoking, miniskirted, partying it up, and *sans*-Pedro because, as she said, "Maybe I won't get a seizure tonight."

Here's hoping, Suzanne.

And yet, as days went by, stories changed. Bob was a crab racer but also a great father; Lil with the big mouth was a true island ambassador; Dawn, the pushy one, was a tough cookie; and Tina, who raged, was a great artist.

We also learned Recovering Ralph was the hardest worker you ever saw; Snorkeling Jeanne was a spiritual seeker; Squatter Jane was an original who kept the old-time island flavor; and Seizure Suzanne was, well, young and trying to find herself.

Meaning, by the time we left, we didn't know the true story about anybody, about who was a good person you could trust, and who to avoid at all costs. Just like back home.

Except those nasty lionfish. Everybody agreed they hated them one and all.

But have you ever seen how beautiful they are?

To wait or not to wait

Wait one minute before you read this. Just sixty seconds. Sixty ... fifty-nine ... fifty-eight ... Can you do it?

My friends from the Netherlands can't do it either. To meet us for a trip, they drove to Amsterdam, flew to Barcelona, took a taxi to a hotel, met us fresh from America, then refused to wait in line for any of the sights we came to see. If their plane had been stuck on the tarmac for two hours like ours was, they would have clawed their seats to shreds, wrapped the oxygen masks around their necks, and downed all the tiny bottles of vodka.

They would not wait for a museum, not wait for plates of tapas, not even wait for the ice-cold sangria that would have made them not care about waiting. To them this is some kind of religion. If the coffee was still brewing in one place, they would walk to another and another until they found cups that were hot and ready. Which could take three hours, but these hours don't count as "waiting" hours, they count as "doing" hours. This, we learned, is part of a different equation that ends up in a different plus and minus column at the end of the day.

Since Ray and I wanted to prove we were open-minded, and didn't want to be flogged and harangued, we agreed to tolerate their fundamentalist dogma. We decided we'd better learn the key tenets of the faith to avoid any unintentional blasphemy.

I received the instructions under the gun of an eyelash curler and mascara. Brigitte was in the middle of a cosmetic activity and asked me to wait a moment for tutelage. That's how I learned Belief Number One: If you are not the "wait-ER," and if blue eye shadow is involved, the event doesn't count as waiting.

Belief Number Two: Four minutes of waiting, like in an ATM line, is comparable to four hours and forty minutes of looking for another machine that has no line.

Belief Number Three: Unused waiting minutes carry over. If you can't find that empty ATM, returning to your hotel safe for cash—which could take two hours but is in the doing category—rewards you with extra waiting minutes for the future. These bonus minutes come in handy if you fall from exhaustion and must endure a marathon nine-hour wait in an emergency room.

Belief Number Four: Choosing an unpopular restaurant with no line that has terrible, inedible food is a *doing* activity. So even if you end up sick as a dog—requiring one of those unfortunate emergency room visits—you would have kept the faith. Sick is preferable to waiting.

Belief Number Five: Almost anything is preferable to waiting, including grossly overpaying, using up lots of pricey gasoline, walking until your shoes rot, choosing from miniscule options, hating your life, and hurling your body in front of a train so you don't need to wait for the next one.

In the spirit of full disclosure, I should admit that for years I've sought membership in the radically different "don't mind waiting" congregation. Instead of blowing a fuse at a checkout counter, I attempt to practice *tadasana,* the yoga mountain pose, standing tall and balanced. Instead of swearing and sweating in a packed doctor's office, I attempt to enter a parallel universe of breathing exercises, *pranayama*, to stay calm.

So, near the end of a busy day, I was breathing full and slow, trying to relax, as the four of us sat at a usually packed café in one of Barcelona's fashionable squares. It was 4:30 in the afternoon. Lunch was long over. Dinner was not for several hours. In fact, the café was officially closed, but the outdoor tables were empty. Lex and Brigitte, our adored Dutch companions, were thrilled to grab one. No lines.

Suddenly, I realized they weren't just sitting there, they were basking in the glory of snatching the ideal table without waiting, even if the only thing on tap was their own bottle of water. Me, I was meditating with my eyes open—long, deep, steady breaths in the diaphragm—peacefully watching them be satisfied they beat the clock. Ray, meantime, was playing captain of our divided ship, chatting away, making a great attempt to keep this group together.

Straying

We weren't paying him any attention. We were all way too occupied keeping the faith in our own sacred congregations.

Shark attack

When the summertime comes, many of us keep our eyes peeled on the waves for that blade of darkness rising from the deep. We watch, we shiver, and we remember *an almost encounter* in the ocean that makes us question why we penetrate the great underwater unknown where we were not born to live.

Everyone has an almost.

An almost swept away by an undertow, an almost full-on collision with something—*What was that?*—an ass-over-elbows tumble that almost left us broken in pieces.

We're not talking about the things that do happen. Hallelujah. We're talking about the things that almost happen, the things that keep us honest when it comes to throwing caution to the wind to plunge into the ocean. So many almosts they hardly count.

Except when it comes to sharks.

Mine was July 2009. It wasn't yesterday and it wasn't in the Atlantic or Pacific, so you may be temporarily safe there. Maybe.

I was lounging on the island of St. Martin while Ray was back at the inn, a bit under the weather. I wasn't nursing him back to health. With all the money we spent on the trip why should both of us suffer? That's obviously where I went wrong. The sharks were coming to make me pay.

The sun glittered on the turquoise water like diamonds, the waves lapped on the silky shore like baby's breath, the palm trees rustled like angel wings. Big teeth—somewhere—chomped.

I put on my mask and fins and headed out for a long swim, tracing the shore so I wouldn't lose my way. A family group drowsed on blankets, children skipped, sand squished.

I swam. One arm over the other—reaching, pulling, gliding—the sea stroking the dorsal spine of the mermaid I was meant to be.

Then ALL HELL BROKE LOOSE.

Hmmm, I thought, as I inhaled and gazed landward, *the beach group is going nuts. Something is happening but what does it have to do with me?*

I swam.

Did I say NUTS? On my next couple of breaths, I saw from my watery distance that the group had risen from its blankets, had made its way to the shoreline, and was waving, frantically.

Hopping, yelling, pointing—at what, to whom?

Now look, I'm used to open water. I've seen scary stuff. I've swum in groups with reef sharks, seals, barracuda. I've been in the water with whales, sea elephants, giant eels. Watching these screamers, all I could think was *stone-cold sissies.*

Then I heard it, faint as a purr yet frantic as a roar: "Get in! Get in! Get in!"

Then I stopped thinking.

In the speed with which a doomed fish vaults out of its slippery home, I swam—thrusting, hurling, gasping—until my heaving body slapped the shore and rolled like cheese filling inside a sand tortilla, flopping on the beach.

Whaaat is happening?

With a collapse of relief, their convulsions stopped. A shark, they said—way bigger than me, two times bigger, three times bigger—was my steady companion the whole time. Its dorsal fin glided next to my dorsal, its sleek back shone in the sun, its dark silhouette was solid against the horizon, and its giant teeth were ready to take a nibble, a bite, to create a gouge, a cavern.

I never saw it. I was looking the other way. There is a God.

No, it probably wouldn't have hurt me if I survived the heart attack from seeing it. Despite awful tragedies, we know shark attacks are rare. This lonely fish would have likely gone its skulking way and I wouldn't have known a thing if my helpers hadn't freaked out on the shore.

Or maybe it would have taken a barely noticeable nibble for him to find out I taste terrible, sending a red calling card far and wide to cold-hearted buddies who would quickly surround me, thus sending that poor beach group into high gear to execute a well-intentioned though likely unsuccessful rescue at sea.

Enough!

No, nothing bad happened. It was another *almost* in the banks of memory that download ever so swiftly—chest pounding, knees buckling, mind racing—with each perilous dive into the murky summer surf.

Happy swimming!

Did I say five times bigger?

How to be a legend

Being hearty like a can of beans at a campfire in the middle of bears, in the middle of a storm, all alone in the wilderness, has always sounded like the kind of girl I want to be.

Enter Josie Brown, or Chuck Norris with female parts.

Josie Brown's not her real name because I can't beat her in a fight. She's a Colorado person I met, the kind who doesn't live near a town or even a Wendy's. When I asked for a dinner recommendation, she said simply, "I don't eat out."

I first saw Josie and her ten-gallon hat on an empty Rocky Mountain highway while I was on a hiking trip. Was she a newer, more modern version of the famous women of the Wild West? Women like Annie Oakley, Belle Starr, Big Nose Kate? There she was hitching a ride after a weekend camping trip carrying a fifty-pound backpack filled with empty wine bottles.

I can tolerate a glass of wine supervised at a bar. Josie Brown can be alone in the wilderness and drink.

I said out loud to my nephew Ethan, who I'd taken on the trip, "If I were a man, I'd marry someone like that. Enough of this skinny, weak, high maintenance model rubbish. Josie Brown's the kind of person you want covering your back, a woman who's more beautiful where it counts, deep in the six-pack abs."

I watched Josie strut toward my car like a cowgirl at a rodeo and remembered working on a ranch myself—which lasted three weeks and four days because I fell in a hole I was digging and broke my foot.

Josie Brown would have broken the neck of the shovel.

"I understand women like that," I said to Ethan, beginning a story I've told a dozen times. "I've been a cowgirl you know.

"I rounded up cattle and drove bulldozers and helped shoe horses and like a Hungry-Man meal, I was quite hearty on that ranch. The manager said I was his best worker."

I didn't tell Ethan it was because I was the only one who showed up on time. The cowhands were always sick drunk.

"I wore cowboy boots and cowboy hats and thick blue jeans with no designer logo and spent nights on the range swapping stories of raging bulls and massive stampedes."

I didn't mention I could barely ride a horse, or that the horse saddle was so heavy it brought me to my knees.

In the back of my mind floated a quote from another famous Wild West woman, Calamity Jane: "I figure if a girl wants to be a legend, she should just go ahead and be one."

I continued.

"And every morning at eight o'clock, no make that four, before the sun come up, I would climb the hayloft, high as a mountain in snow, and stick that pitchfork plumb into a fat bundle and fling it one-handed right on target to a flatbed truck below."

I didn't mention I would fall backward along with the bale.

"Then we'd take off and drive cattle."

I didn't mention the guys gave me jobs like rounding up lost cows, or sweeping old hay, or fixing fences in the way back forty, then ditched me to hitch back home myself.

But, like Calamity Jane, I was determined, meaning I was dumb. Calamity Jane got herself into lots of trouble in the Wild West and so did I that Colorado summer.

"And that broken foot, it coulda happened to anyone," I said to Ethan. "That hole I dug was six foot if it was an inch and it was damn lucky I didn't end up a goner. A giant wind come up and the whole state was reeling this way and that. I tell ya, I was between here and the Good Lord."

I puffed myself up behind the steering wheel, pointed my finger in Ethan's face, and said, "You pick someone like that!" Then I straightened my red baseball cap, cocked my head, and went eyeball-to-eyeball with Josie Brown as she stood with her hitching thumb still out.

"Howdy pardner," I nodded. "Nice weather, ain't it? Looks like you're fixin' for a beer and a ride."

True confessions
with strangers

There's no better place than a half-naked environment far from home to share your deepest, darkest secrets. Before you know it, people say things. Lots of things. Forbidden things. Take, for example, the hotel hot tub.

With warm water caressing you, bubbles blocking your sight, and you resting secure in the knowledge you'll never see these people again, God willing, it's the perfect environment for true confessions. And thankfully when your inner bubbly has been spilled—maybe you hate your job or your mate or you wish you could relocate far from your wretched family—everyone dries off and tiptoes far, far away.

You hope.

So there we were, two guys and three girls, soaking away, when one woman blurted, "I've never had any confidence in myself." Right in the middle of a fine hotel in Havana, steam rising, she admitted she wasn't seeing square with the new boyfriend who was soaking up another kind of liquid at the hotel bar. Pretty soon the hot tub was a hot bed of revelation: "I don't think I'm such a good mother," said one. "I haven't made a new friend in twenty years," said another. "I'm stressed out like a zebra in a pack of hyenas," a third chimed in. One personal stick of dynamite after another while the sun set and the next thing you knew, the five of us were bonded like plaque in an artery.

This was the time to tiptoe away, leaving it all to fizzle. But then Lucy, our self-proclaimed control freak, exclaimed, "We'll never see each other again. Come on, there are only hours to go. Let's get it all off our chests."

And in the spirit of what happens at Motel 6 stays there, we obeyed. Masochists, every last one of us.

We met again at the hotel club. No-confidence Janelle and her soon-to-be-dumped Jim were smoking. In the thrill of the over-sharing, I-can-do-better moment, she announced, "This is my last cigarette, and his, too." Then she pointed in the silent prisoner's direction. The Marlboro man, waving his glowing stick, was trapped like a zebra: "*Whaaat?*"

We descended like hyenas: "Do it, do it, do it, do it ... "

Meanwhile, controlling Lucy wanted to learn to jump into something, anything, because she was an over-planner. Ryan was a loner, someone else was wishy-washy, someone else a perfectionist. Then there was the lazy dude, the scaredy cat, the rationalizer, the one who lived perilously close to the edge.

By three in the morning, the latest I'd stayed up in a decade, we'd left our layers of griminess all over the poor Cuban hotel. Janelle and Jim backed away from the abyss of being smoke-free half a dozen times: "We were just joking, we didn't mean it, we were getting into the spirit of the moment."

We threatened to send drones. We were feisty and we wanted other people to do things we couldn't do ourselves.

By four in the morning, we all admitted we had work to do—*I mean who doesn't?*—then we laughed and kissed and hugged and inched toward our rooms, but that wasn't enough. Lucy was determined to round us up for the kill.

"We have to hold ourselves accountable," she demanded. "Contact information, come on, right now." She was our true hyena, adorably young. We were caught.

I'm not going to admit my true confessions of that long evening, because I know you people and those people I didn't know. Except we didn't count on social media-obsessed Lucy. She made us form a WhatsApp group to keep us honest.

People these days!

Whatever happened to reveling in the comfort of strangers, saying any dumb thing you want, calling a night a night, then going on your merry, dysfunctional way?

Set your photos free

When Ray goes somewhere, anywhere, he has a large DSLR in one hand and an extra point-and-shoot in the other in case the big picture shows up on the Pacific while he's focused on the Atlantic.

Plus, there are multiple camera lenses, a tripod, a monopod, assorted waist and shoulder bags, extra batteries, extra memory cards. To top off the look, he wears a multi-pocketed vest that makes him look like a cross between Indiana Jones, a Greek fisherman, a coupon redeemer at Bed Bath & Beyond, and an older and less flirty version of Ashton Kutcher taking photographs instead of just picking up chicks.

With all this paraphernalia along for the trip, I long ago stopped dragging my own 35mm camera when my red fashion-accessory Nikon crashed and split. Give me a technical device and you run the serious risk of seeing it dismembered right before your eyes.

Truth is, I'm an anti-photographer.

Ray's theory: see it, love it, see it again in the comfort of your own home.

My theory: see it, love it, set it free. Free is not living inside a heap of plastic or pleading from inside a picture frame.

Despite my wet blanket attitude, I know a great thing when I see it. And our trip to Machu Picchu was going to be a great thing, so even I packed a tiny camera just in case Ansel Adams Kutcher was in the wrong place at the wrong time, and it was up to me to return home with the proof.

So there I was in the Inca ruins having a darn good time and making a record of it. I avoided the hard shots: the intricate details of the architecture, the wrinkled Andean women in their wide Crayola-colored skirts, the grinning mountain kids. Instead, I focused on the stuff I couldn't destroy because it was too picture perfect. Like all of Machu Picchu.

Suddenly, I was looking at the world the way photographers do, with a big barrier of glass that prevents any real connection. Wait, I take it back. That was the old me. The new me, weapon in hand, was seeing things in a way no one had ever seen before. The colors, the shapes, the misinterpreted angles, the hidden meanings all appeared before my lens as if waiting for the right person to reveal the true depth of the Inca civilization.

When we got home, the camera buff disappeared into his office to become one with his Photoshop software. I knew this meant he was doing things that make older women look bad. If real life can be enhanced to look more enticing, what chance does a fading female have of accepting herself without plastic surgery?

And yet, like a good facelift, the results were hard to argue with. I was invited to a showing with popcorn because he wanted me to linger and fawn. But wait, something was missing.

Me: Where are the photos I dropped on your desk to be uploaded? Where are my shots of the famous Sun Temple, the sacred mountains, the gods that I swear appeared to me in flesh and blood?

Ray: Well, better hold onto your popcorn, this is going to be a bumpy ride.

In other words, was that Machu Picchu in the clouds or maybe an anthill encircled in white spider webs? Was that a llama grazing on the terraced land, or maybe a deer chewing bushes in my own front yard?

"The Inca empire wasn't built in a day," I huffed, and retired to my own office after slamming my camera back on the shelf. But first I removed the memory card to set my rotten images free.

Then, after Ray went to bed, I snuck back to his office and marveled—in the comfort of my own home—at the wonders we had seen and the wonders we could see over and over again.

Saying goodbye to my suitcase

When Macy's had a sale—the kind of offer you can't refuse—I decided to send my old suitcase to the graveyard of high-tech nylon and inner mesh pockets. I bought a spanking new Travelpro that—*you know*—rolls faster than a speeding bullet, is stronger than a locomotive, and leaps tall escalators in a single bound.

Then I marched to the attic and dragged out the worn, tattered, beaten, battered Ricardo I'd been lugging for fifteen years. I parked it on the sidewalk next to the bathroom trash and leftover dinner. Then I strutted back to the house slapping one hand triumphantly against the other. *Good riddance. I'm done with that baby.*

I could see it from my window, waiting like a lost sock, a single shoe, a lone teddy bear left dirty and useless. Waiting, as it did so many times, waiting for me. It looked like a broken-down hooker needing one last fling. After so many years of flat-on-its-back service, could I simply toss it aside for a younger piece of virgin plastic?

I rolled it back to the house, realizing it deserved a proper goodbye.

Dear Suitcase,

You followed me everywhere like a dedicated soldier. I can hardly say that about anything or anyone. I was the leader; you were the follower. No matter how fast I buzzed through airports, you stayed with me, you rolled while I ran. Loyal as you were, yet big and bulbous, sometimes you embarrassed me. I wanted to pretend you weren't mine. Still, you stayed true blue, sturdy and stout, as I paid extra at airport check-in because you held so darn much.

I stuffed you like a poor goose, bumped you down steps, kicked you forward, pulled you back, sat on you, slept on you, yelled at you because I wanted to be free of you. Once I almost threw you over a hill, though you steadfastly held every single thing I needed. If you'd been lost, I'd have been lost, too.

You followed me surer than a show dog at Westminster, despite no training, no treats, no pats, no warm bed. You were manhandled, suffocated, left shivering in the corner of a chilly, soulless cargo hold while I flew high and mighty above you. Then you did it again and again and again.

You were rerouted to places I'd never been while I, a madwoman stuck in a smelly outfit, paced frantically looking for you. Once I thought about nothing but you for days, talked about nothing but you, wanted nothing but you, until you faithfully reappeared in charge of every wrinkled T-shirt I owned.

I was so happy to see you, I cried. In your own rugged way, I think you cried, too. Was that a new tear on your plastic rim, or a salty tear from the rim of your hidden eye?

You are the most worldly, helpful object I've ever had. And in your voiceless way, you know things. Who stole my jean jacket out of you in Marrakech, how it felt to have your body shrink-wrapped in Johannesburg so no creep would put their hands inside of you, how dizzying it is to circle round and round the carousel, hoping some stranger won't mistake you for her own.

You know, old friend, as I gaze at you upright and rolling but well scuffed and frayed, I wonder if you still have a few more journeys left? I must admit, I've got some serious scuffs of my own.

Tell you what. How about I put you next to the new guy, and maybe you can teach that top ace what really goes on in the luggage hold, how you won those scars, year after year, mile after mile.

Stay ready and able, my friend. I have a feeling any day now, for old times' sake, you and I—two of a well-worn kind—will go a-travelin'.

Layer Five:
Reconciling

Practice, practice, practice. In the studio or on the page. Here we go again. As we say in yoga, another day, another downward facing dog, *adho mukha svanasana*. Start on all fours, lift your hips high, take them back, strengthen your arms and legs, press your chest toward your knees, extend your head upside down. Go for it!

Or as we say in writing: sit your derrière in the chair.

In both cases, you apply effort, intention, integrity, then add a huge dose of acceptance.

The other side of practice—or *abhyasa* in yoga—is called *vairagya*, loosely defined as detachment, as letting go. You practice hard as you can, with dedication, with vigor, with zeal, then you remember the target is bigger than today. It's about becoming a better version of yourself, a person who connects to a deeper sense of wisdom free from grasping, someone who tries to do their best. What else can life ask?

With humility and patience, step-by-step, moment-by-moment, you confront the mental chaos and work to embody a state of unshakable peace. At least that's your plan, and as we learned as kids, it's good to have plans otherwise we'd never get anything done at all.

Little by little, day by day, you're becoming the yogi delicately perched on a lotus flower, legs entwined in *padmasana,* floating serene, finally willing—*whew*—to move into acceptance of what is.

Unless, of course, you're late for a writing deadline or a class tromping in the door.

Your decision-making guide

The women in my longtime support group, the Wisdom
Divas, are sick and tired of managing their own lives.
Should we, or shouldn't we? Do we, or don't we? Or
worse yet—did we, or didn't we?

To get to the bottom of the problem, we plunged into
the concept of "maximizers versus satisficers"—one of the
popular models for coming to conclusions when faced with
different paths, as poet Robert Frost wrote a hundred years
ago: "Two roads diverged in a yellow wood."

"You could do better," is the maximizer's manic
mantra. "A bird in the hand is worth two in the bush," is
the sweet song of satisficers who believe good enough is
the new perfect.

Let's clarify. "Satisficers"—a strange word for the saner
of the two groups—are people who identify maybe three
top criteria essential for a quick, painless decision. Then
they get crackin'. For example, you're buying a hat and
your demands are:

1. In my price range
2. Matches my outfit
3. Makes me look cool

Satisficers would say they're content if they hit the list, even if they blow the fit. Another demand, like size, could put them on the slippery slope of maximizers, people who engage in head-banging obsession on every issue, say a hat, down to the last band and brim.

Surely though, I'm not the first to notice it's the day after a satisfying choice that the floodgates open and a slew of maximum dream options roll in.

Yet even then, maximizers could be unhappy with the dream. They spend so much time weighing pros and cons that when they're already in the dress, in the chapel, on the boat, those pesky cons still circle their brains like vultures looking for a tasty meal.

Deciding how to decide, it seems, is as hard as deciding.

The Wisdom Divas, as our name implies, are supposed to know these things, but don't judge a people by their brand.

Diva 1: It's so embarrassing but deciding where to travel drives me nuts. Fiji or Kansas? Such a toss-up!

Diva 2: I can't decide if I should stay in my relationship. Am I supposed to enjoy being with him?

Diva 3: If I decide to take that bigger job, I'll never have time to see my family. Is that a good thing?

We sigh.

Reconciling

Since we clearly need help—and since we think embracing satisfaction is the adult way to go—we start practicing our three top criteria.

For example, in the case of finding a mate, we could propose:

1. A man who stands upright
2. A man who can afford a cup of coffee
3. A man who snores only occasionally

But what if the day after you become a satisficer and settle for this kind of simple man, you meet one who can fly you first class to Europe? And you think he's sexy. And he likes to talk about relationships. Those are three better things right there. Why not start out with those three things?

Obviously, we want it all: peace, exhilaration, love. Those are three things. Yet when it comes to decision-making, sometimes we get another three things: confusion, wasted time, exhaustion.

Maybe it's not our fault. Plenty has been written about what Robert Frost had in his mind when he wrote "The Road Less Taken." It's possibly the most popular American poem in history, yet also the most misunderstood. Perhaps, Frost meant it as a joke to a wishy-washy friend, or he intended to spark the great spirit of American individualism, or he simply wrote it as an ode to the intriguing twists and turns of a winding forest.

Those are three things.

Really, if we're still wondering all these years later what criteria Frost had in his mind, how can we ever stand at that fork in the road without banging our heads against the trees until the whole forest falls down?

The whole messy truth

This story is about a divorced man, a sink, a cookie, and a few questions.

The man, a plumber, was chatting about his life as tradesmen tend to do when surrounded by the intimacy of early morning, a scantily dressed female, an emergency, and soggy waste.

He asked the first question: "How long has the sink been leaking?"

I asked the second question while he was installing a new kitchen faucet, which had sprung a geyser that morning. He had already told me about the daughter nearby, the first grandchild, the ex-wife who lived hours away.

"So," I said, "you're a confirmed bachelor now?"

His head bobbed up and down, his arms swept sideways in defeat, and he bellowed, "Yes."

Which I thought was a shame. He was cute in that down-to-earth, unassuming kind of way that makes you think of work benches, camping, and falling asleep with a beer on the couch.

Me: Because …?

Plumber: Because I can't get along with anybody.

We laughed.

He didn't say his wife was a cheater, or no longer the woman he married, or that she didn't appreciate his hidden talents, his penchant for dirty jobs, his sexy slip of the ol' pants when reaching underneath a broken sink. None of that.

He told the truth, maybe not the whole messy truth, but something real. He said if you took a good, hard look at him, you'd see he wasn't much of a catch.

And suddenly, I found him very attractive.

Me: But you're so cute.

He blushed. And winked.

Ray unexpectedly peeked around the corner to check if I was flirting. I figure if you get to be a certain age, men know you're joking. Ray disagrees. "Watch it," he likes to say. "You're not that old."

I continued to chat but backed away, just a little. Just in case.

Me: So you're too difficult to live with, set in your ways, can't compromise?

Plumber: Yeah, I'm all those things. I'm impossible. It's better to leave me alone.

So he was flawed. So what? Who isn't? I was charmed that he didn't make up a story, throw a curve ball, make his ex the bad guy. Maybe he was on to something. If this plumber in his smeared shirt and padded knees could get a

tell that to Margaret-Rosario. She told me her name once and gave me a condescending nod when I asked if I'd gotten it right. Then I was supposed to say the entire seven syllables with all the other Tims, Toms, Kates, and Dicks I have to remember. And who knows—the next time I see her she might be a Margaret-Rosario-Katarina-Alison-Maude, or she might have gone in the opposite direction and become a plain old Peg.

I don't want to accuse other people of name obsession and not admit my own. I sort of have two first names, and people often call me Debby. I remember every person who's done it. Yup, I keep a list.

To get over it, I've rebranded myself, too. Picking up on a celebrity trend—who can stop me—I'm now a letter: D. Or you can think of it as a sound: D.

Your choice. I'm absolutely flexible.

So long as you get it right.

Who needs talent to sing?

I can't sing.

Sure, I can open my mouth and belt out a few tuneless lines, but I always assumed singing meant more than a chaotic shrieking with no resemblance to the song Alexa is blasting on the speaker.

At least, I assumed.

To explore this topic, let's look up the definition of singing, shall we? Oxford says, "making musical sounds with the voice." Merriam-Webster adds, "to utter with musical inflections." Musical, meantime, is defined as "having a pleasant sound."

Quite restrictive, I might argue, with little room for personal interpretation.

Merriam-Webster also uses the definition "to celebrate in verse." But I've heard no champagne pop, no hands clap, when I sing along with Lady Gaga to "Born This Way." Unfair, because I *was* born this way—no ear, no pitch—and I maintain compassionate exception should be given to me and all the other off-key crooners.

Even those rare times I do open my mouth, my Alexa often goes kaput.

As a loud child, before the world had its way with me, I had the guts to sing in my outside voice in school assemblies with songs like "My Favorite Things" from *The Sound of Music*, and "Wouldn't it be Loverly" from *My Fair Lady*. I sang full-throttle, fearless, so exuberantly, so unaware in my Julie Andrews fan euphoria, that my teacher—with her eyes bugged out and a finger over pursed lips—suggested that I should, "Turn down the volume."

I was so horrified, so embarrassed, I've rarely sung in public again. Ever. Yet I know the words to songs. Lots of songs. Cosmic mismatch? Cue the violins.

Not everyone is so scarred. At a recent dinner party, another individualist, also born this way, opened her mouth to piano accompaniment. And this was definitely a voice of note that couldn't keep a note, not a "favorite thing" or a "loverly" voice. There was no question the human ability to fully stretch every inch of vocal cord was in progress.

She plain old wailed.

And clearly loved every thunderous moment of it.

So did I. She didn't hurt my ears. She opened my eyes.

Her body shook, her curly hair stood on end, the glasses in the cabinets rattled, the lights flickered. Her sheer enjoyment helped us all have a rollicking moment letting our voices out. And we all know that means more than just singing.

Obviously, this wayward diva hadn't gotten the same childhood message I did. Instead of "Turn down the volume," she must have heard, "Sweet darlin,' you let the whole darn world know you're alive, and you spread your brand of joy far and wide. Don't pay any attention to what other folks think."

She never said she was auditioning for Broadway. She was singing for the fun of it.

Was that allowed?

A bit of research later, I learned singing improves mental and physical health *even if* you're not good at it. Why isn't that *even if* in the dictionary?

Singing reduces stress, boosts immunity, increases lung function, helps manage grief, may improve snoring, and most marvelously, revs up a sense of belonging and connection with those wailing right along with you.

But you singers already know this.

The next day, sitting at my firepit with a few friends and classic rock in the background, I did the unthinkable. I used my outside voice—not on the inside like when I'm alone with Alexa—but on the outside.

Usually, I would feed people the words then take a lonely backseat. Not this time.

I spread my arms wide like Julie Andrews in *The Sound of Music*, and I howled. Tone deaf or not, I moved from "Born This Way" to "Born to Be Wild."

Be forewarned.

Natural Botox

When I showed my old friend Ellen the bronze "vegan leather" bomber jacket I bought on sale at Bloomingdale's, she said emphatically, "That's you."

She didn't mean it fit me, or the color was right, or even that it looked great. That would be way too superficial for someone who's known me since I was fourteen. She meant it looked like the "me" she knows on the inside though the outside is now a whole different story.

"Too old for an edgy bomber jacket?" I asked.

"Absolutely not," she replied.

My face perked up ten or twenty years.

Old friends like Ellen can be as rejuvenating as an exfoliation or a cruise. She knows things about me I would never under any circumstances tell another living soul. Except maybe all of you because I know you people can keep a secret.

In fact, it's a huge relief to admit in black and white that, despite my feeble attempts to change, I have some of the same defects I had as a teenager. For example, I have the sense of direction of a pot, but even a pot has the brains to have someone else carry it around.

Most people point this out to me on a regular basis, but Ellen does not. She just laughs. Not at me, but with me. She thinks it's funny. It reminds her of crazy things we did like hitchhike in Spain with me standing on the wrong side of the road, my thumb hanging out.

Or the time I drove us in the wrong direction on Philadelphia's six-lane Roosevelt Boulevard, stopping three lanes of oncoming traffic and nearly causing a multi-vehicle calamity. I blamed everyone else: "Who taught these people how to drive?"

Ellen—my teenage ego booster, partner in crime, and cheerleader compadre (we were both in our blue and gold outfits, pom-poms in the back seat)—never disagreed.

Ellen was in the passenger seat again when we navigated the treacherous waters of a funeral procession. No one close, thank goodness, though by the time we got there one of us being a corpse was a real possibility.

Funeral processions demand a great deal of organized attention. Even before we slipped into my car, Ellen gave me one of those sideways glances people throw at you when they know you're in the driver's seat, in this case literally, yet fear you have no idea what you're doing. When she got done praying, you could see the wheels turning as she plotted a strategy that would somehow end at the burial site for her distant relation before the spirits themselves called it a night.

So there we were in a long line of cars, ready to pass stop signs, ignore red lights, and frantically brake and start. There's this whole jerky protocol to the sedate funeral procession, everyone following in a confused, hurrying frenzy to get to the sacred, solemn event for someone who is in no rush at all to lie in the same place forever. All without U-turns, backtracking, a makeup correction, a coffee break or two, or asking a dozen people for directions.

It's a recipe for my worst nightmare—especially because we were the last car in line since I couldn't figure out how to get in line in the first place.

"Help!" I yelled. "We're losing them!"

But Ellen didn't yell back. She didn't even accuse me of not having evolved at all since the last time I almost killed her on the road. That's history. She just guided me forward like a calm navigator stuck with a stormy captain: stop, go, turn right, look up, step on it, turn left, get your foot on the brake, the brake, the brake, the BRAKE!

Maybe she feared this was her final moment. But in my book, she was taking control because old girlfriends know when you're doing the best you can. They also know when the two of you, together, somehow combine to make one solid functioning adult. She's always hated to drive, but she's always gotten me to our destination.

I once saw a sign that read: "Friends pick you up when you're down. But good friends push you back down and make you laugh."

And Ellen did make me laugh. When the day was over,

we doubled over in the car like two teenagers out of the house on a Friday night. It was a shot of old girlfriend Botox.

But it didn't cost a cent. And more importantly—if our stars are aligned better than a bad sense of direction—it should last us both a lifetime.*

*Or nearly a lifetime. Ellen died in 2018, and I knew I needed someone steady to drive me to the funeral.

Drivel

Since no one has asked me to deliver a commencement speech—an obvious oversight—I'd like to offer the advice I'd share if ever called to whittle down life into one neat package.

Forget the top ten. Who has time? How about the top one? What's the one thing you'd say to every anxious, confused, hopeful, promising young person that would help them sail through life a little taller, a little happier, maybe even a little longer?

After sifting through layers of wisdom painfully earned and heroically recounted by speakers to future generations, I'd like to add this to the conversation: Stand up and be counted. No matter how wacky you are.

The thought reared its sagacious head after one shy grad complained about a difficult classmate she couldn't confront on a final school project.

"I have a hard time asserting myself," she admitted. "I just don't know how to do it."

Welcome to the club.

After trying to have a peaceful lunch while sitting next to a phone-shouting, table-hugging guy, I felt her pain.

Although I was there first—*I called it first!*—I was unable to suggest he take his silly nonsense somewhere else, like Indonesia. I, too, on that day, was unable to stand up and be counted.

The same thing happened a few days earlier when I did not know how, couldn't quite get the right tone of voice, when I tried to react to a grump who didn't acknowledge my friendly greeting in a hallway. Such a tiny thing, yet it stuck in my chest like mud.

I wanted to say, "Excuse me, HELLO!" but I didn't.

The moments of not standing up mount. Yesterday, today, tomorrow.

My advice: Get it over with. Start young to claim your itty-bitty plot of earth. I didn't say that to the shy grad though, so I need to yank it off my tight chest and say it to you.

Instead of blabbering to some poor family hostage about all the things we coulda said, how about keeping it light, direct, and easy from the start? How about "Get a room," which I wish I'd delivered to an amorous couple at the gym hot tub. Or "Could you shrink over one seat, Lincoln?" to a tall gentleman who blocked my view in a movie theater. Or "Of course you can eat all my spring rolls, but first let me douse them in hot sauce."

Something sweet and caring.

If the words are trying to bust out and you won't spark an international incident—which is not a given but maybe you have to try anyway, because chest tightness could lead to something quite serious—gather up your courage and SAAAY IT!

But I didn't tell this to the grad because, well, because I didn't. Because sometimes, even as a full-fledged adult, in the moment I just don't know how.

But short of starting a riot, I should have suggested she experiment. Start small. Send back bad food at a restaurant; face a stranger who cuts in line; confront a grungy roommate unless that's you. Then see if you can move up to speak to the friend who dissed you, the lazy coworker, the lame boyfriend or girlfriend, the mean boss.

Sure, there may be times to avoid, to put on sunglasses and earphones, for safety's sake, for time's sake. But when you truly have something on your mind, I should have said to the grad, you better stake out your rightful plot of earth before someone else builds a house on it.

Start young. Stand up. Be nice. Be polite. Be fair. Be counted. Duck when necessary.

Look, maybe the one piece of advice you'd give wide-eyed young people is rejected as drivel. That may well be the case. But at least—for one brief wondrous moment—it's not their confused, tormented, agonizing drivel that we listen to again and again and again.

Amen.

A great big whoosh

I f you're not the type to bare all, never had a great bikini or Speedo body, yet still want to feel light and airy during long, warm days, take a cue from the intimidating snake.

No, that's not a euphemism for your last boy or girlfriend. I'm talking about the garter snake or perhaps the poisonous copperhead that left its skin sitting in my woodpile. I discovered it as I dragged out the last logs for the final fires of winter.

Whatever kind of snake it was, it was cozy enough to drop its drawers outside of my house. It must have felt glorious in its cold-blooded heart, free, complete, done, before it crept off to scare somebody half to death.

In reality, the snake has nothing on us; it sheds its crinkly layer a handful of times a year. We get a new top skin every month. And every hour, see it or not, maybe 40,000 tiny skin cells slough off, shreds of dust, a scarcely noticeable reduction in wrinkles, pockmarks, unsightly moles, and hideous scars.

Inspired by the reptile and sensing spring in the air, I decided to look for ways a human being can experience that same big whoosh.

I started cleaning. I threw away old flannel nightgowns, torn T-shirts, faded gym tights. I gathered dresses that never fit, shoes that pinch, filled a new bag for Goodwill. I shook out rugs, wiped down woodwork. I picked up dead branches in the yard, tossed away broken slate.

I got a new haircut, shorter, bouncier. I brightened my teeth, ready to smile for spring. I exfoliated 'til I throbbed.

I wanted more.

I thought deeper, remembering the snake may be considered mean, backstabbing, untrustworthy, but in the spirit world it's the symbol of transformation, rebirth, healing. *What do you need to shake off?* it asks in its hissing, coiling, gutsy way, challenging us to leave our scraps behind in one fell swoop.

"Metamorphosis," I said out loud to the sky, "that's what I want." I threw up my hands and stated my willingness to change, put a new stake in the ground. I vowed to let go of old ways I know clear as daylight do not serve me well: pride, indecision, fear—crusts that keep growing back, that don't easily break off.

I held up what the snake left behind, pale and crackly, happy my home served as a winter retreat for this hearty reptile. I thanked it for giving me a kick in the epidermis, a reason to ponder how to greet the new season with a shake and a wiggle myself, open to the fresh and unspoiled.

I read more about my symbolic friend and learned if you're thinking of a new path but hesitate, the guiding snake supports your efforts, gives you strength, courage.

Conversely, the snake is also said to warn you of moving too fast into something that may not be right.

Suddenly, I was confused.

Was my magical teacher inching me out of my safe protective sheath, or was that bit of fear dripping out of my pores a sign it was not yet time to fling headlong into a shiny new dawn?

That confounding snake!

I laid its remnants in the still chilly garden and was grateful my skin, like my guest's, would continue to cast off the old and be renewed, giving me endless opportunities for evolution. I would continue to try, to slither on, and hopefully not scare too many people along the way.

Marriage or an affair?

We all have lots of opportunities to consider whether a situation will be short-term or long. Maybe it's a relationship or a significant purchase. Perhaps you're pondering an investment of time and energy. Will it be right for a week, a month, a season, a lifetime?

Or just a couple of drinks?

In other words, is it a marriage or an affair?

For example, a house. You'll probably sleep there a few good years, maybe even with the same people, so deciding based on "I just love it" is foolhardy if it's thirty miles from Starbucks, Wegmans, and Bloomie's.

Yet isn't loving something in that wild and silly way the thing that puts the pop in your step, the glow in your sallow cheeks?

And if you're past the age when your cheeks glow, can you recapture that burst of bold abandon in the everyday meanderings of what to eat for dinner, what coat to buy, where to go on a Saturday night?

With choices circling constantly, some harder and riskier than others, I began to raise that piercing question on some pricey acquisitions: Is this a marriage or an affair?

I started with the purchase of two big items, a couch and a car. I also asked the question about designer jeans, but everyone knows long-loving blues are harder to snag than a lifelong mate.

But many selections cause nearly as much distress, which could be solved by pausing then posing: "Will this be a final passage on the road of life or just a passing fancy?"

To figure it out, I wrote two lists.

Marriage:
- ✓ Practical
- ✓ Compatible
- ✓ Not shocking
- ✓ Sort of matches with everything
- ✓ Might be hard to get out of
- ✓ Could lead to pain and suffering

Affair:
- ✓ Flashy
- ✓ Risky
- ✓ Might shock and embarrass
- ✓ Might not match
- ✓ Might be able to get out easy
- ✓ Could lead to pain and suffering

With these ideas in mind, I went couch shopping. I figured beige, the color no one sees, was safe. It's sensible, it horrifies no one, and it matches everything.

Or I could go with neon orange. Flashy, exciting, the boost in youthful riskiness could be worth it, and in a pinch there's Craigslist. Maybe, I realized, it's a long engagement, something between a marriage and a fling. Perhaps a beige couch with neon pillows.

How about buying a car? The sturdy, comfortable mom car, or the speedy, jazzy one with the flat seat and hard headrest? Will its novelty fade with each bump? Or will the joy of being in my affair zone thrill me even if my back hurts and I have a faint headache?

I tried to get clear about what's what, hoping this would create more angst-free shopping.

Sandals are an affair. Easy come, easy go. Hiking boots are a marriage. It takes a long time to break them in. Travel: an affair. There's always the next time. A dress for a wedding: a marriage. The pictures never go away. Nail polish: an affair. A good place to go crazy. A classic black coat: a marriage, or a long engagement if you add a red scarf. Tickets to the theater: an affair. You can skip out at intermission. A midriff top: a one-nighter. A small handbag: a brief fling. A big roomy satchel with space for a water bottle, antacids, lunch, a change of clothes, a Home Depot return: definitely a marriage with children.

Back to the car conundrum. It's not like it's an arm or a leg, an old family expression, though it could cost one or both. Still, it's more than an affair, nearly a marriage.

And it dawned on me, *could I get it all?* Throw caution to the wind but avoid the pain and suffering if it doesn't work out? Get the flashy car, have the wild affair, sign on the dotted line, but not marry it? A little risk, a little shock, a little commitment, then consign it like blue jeans?

And this is why—in these times of too many choices, too much confusion, too much fear, and so much obsession with freedom—living together first and leasing a vehicle are so darn popular.

See yourself as others see you

One of my greatest wishes is to see myself as others see me. To step outside myself, spin around, and gaze straight at the real me in all my radiant splendor or ragged inferiority. Then I would know all the things I should change. Since this is impossible, at least until the technology becomes available, I'm left to trial and error.

But if I could see myself as others see me, in an instant I would know how to change my look, my speech, my walk, my attitude, even how to cut my vegetables to exude an air of casual confidence and enviable attractiveness. Obviously, I need this information desperately, but thus far I've been unable to figure out how to get it.

How can I catch a glimpse of the real me?

Sometimes, to trick myself, I jump out of bed and run to the mirror like I'm in the midst of a dire emergency, which seems to happen quite often. Then I whistle and give a sideways peek to catch what impression I'm making. It's as effective as thinking about floating down a river on a raft with a beer at the same time a dentist is injecting Novocain into an upper back molar.

I know there's much to learn if I could get this. Once, when my father had gained weight and was walking down the hall after a nap, my sister Caryl and I caught his belly sagging below his belt. We grabbed the Polaroid camera, snapped a picture, and presented it to him as he staggered half asleep. He never got chubby again.

In that split second between wakefulness and sleep, and with the evidence presented in black and white, a part of his brain saw the truth before his ego announced, "I must have hunched over for a second" or "Pictures make you look ten pounds heavier."

I once saw myself as others see me and didn't realize it was me. I was strolling mindlessly past a lobby-length hotel mirror and saw a woman moving at exactly the same speed and in exactly the same direction. It continued for what felt like minutes. I walked, she walked, I walked, she walked, and I almost feared I was being followed and had the urge to scream. I looked at her and thought, *She keeps up a nice, smooth pace. I like that about her.* When I realized it was me, I had lost the moment. *Nice, smooth pace* was all the information I gathered.

Hearing yourself as others do is also tough. For example, I have a relative who snores like a jackhammer. He doesn't hear it, so he's convinced he doesn't make a sound, like that tree in the woods. His wife and kids planted a tape recorder under his bed, played back what sounded like a herd of snorting buffalo, but he still didn't believe them. Even if his head bangs on his chest in the middle of a sitting-up snore, his eyes pop open, and his ears are ringing, he'll insist the sound came from the heater.

If I could walk a mile in someone else's moccasins, it's said, I could truly understand them. And if I could gaze at myself with crystal-clear eyes, I could instantly grasp what others say: I do hold my head cocked to one side; I laugh too loud; I move too fast; chewing gum is not a good look.

The list is pathetically long.

But how do I know others are right? And if I see myself as others see me, would I feel compelled to become what others want me to become, and change the way others want me to change? Would that involve letting go not only of the habits, but the realities that may have spawned them: the broken bones, the assorted failures, the family quirks?

I may be okay with dumping those, but the time I danced solo on a baby grand piano in a packed Caribbean bar and developed lifelong bragging rights? That one I'm going to fight for, every bump and grind.

The bird and the worm go at it

One day, I was walking in a field and came upon a small green worm contorting, bending, and struggling as it climbed a tall oak tree. The tiny creature was but a foot off the ground when I saw it begin its heroic journey to the high branch above. Turning and twisting and craning and crawling along the thinnest silk thread hanging from the mighty oak.

The worm, destined to perhaps lay its eggs or fill its belly with the sweet broad leaves above, would not be deterred by the tall measure of its journey. It crept upward, arching its smooth back, propelling forward with all the power its slight, flexible form could muster.

From time to time its strength wavered, and it hung depleted. I feared its admirable task would end, yet soon its thin body mounted again for the fight.

I thought hard about releasing the poor thing from its arduous journey. Cutting it down with the briefest wave of my hand and letting it relax on the soft ground below.

But was I the worm's keeper, its maker? Could I understand the mysterious voyage of this delicate being, to decide whether it should be earthbound or airborne? Should I interrupt its courageous quest?

I watched and offered that small thing the full strength of my encouragement, my fists pumping the air, my voice calling its name, shepherding it on its journey.

"Go, Small Thing, you can do it. All of us, you and I and all the creatures of the earth have done this, have wrestled, have reached far beyond what anyone could have imagined, and we have succeeded. We've traveled unfathomable distances like beggars with nothing but flimsy sandals on our feet.

"Travel upward, Small Thing. You can do it, I can do it, we can do it. For all aspiring creatures, travel on."

That is what I said on that happy summer day, as I marveled at the many miracles of the world we could find in our backyards, on the beaches, in the mountains.

Measure by measure I watched that simple animal climb, cheering it on. Six inches from a high branch it dangled, so near the fragrant leaves bending and swaying that sent waves of sweet promise in the worm's aching direction.

This is where *Aesop's Fables* come in. Do you recall reading them as a kid, those ancient Greek stories that were more hard truth than fairy tale? Stories like "The Goose with the Golden Eggs," "The Ant and the Grasshopper," "The Hare and the Tortoise." Some were tough to swallow.

Some gave us life lessons we never forgot, like that slow tortoise winning the race.

Meantime, remember our little worm? Climbing, crawling, striving. Will it reach that branch? Measure by measure by measure?

Suddenly—on that day, in that place, as this modern story unfolded—an ordinary brown bird swooped in on a journey of its own, snatching the twisting thing in its hungry beak and whisking it away.

The worm would not be tough to swallow.

I stared, crestfallen.

I watched that bird perched on the ground, the dangling heroic slimy thing hanging from its beak, a captured prisoner. My pumping fists dangled as well.

What did this mean for all striving creatures?

If the worm was me, what did this mean for me? If the worm was the symbol of the struggle of the whole world, what did this mean for the whole wide world?

And that is your summer tale for today, folks.

Unless you'd rather see the events from the vantage point of the bird, nibbling and nourishing in the fresh green grass, its feathery wings rustling in the warm air. For that little bird, it was quite a banner moment.

Happy tales, my friends, no matter how you spin them, as nature—season by season, miracle by mystery, story by story—drenches us in wonder.

Me, myself, and I

Apparently, there's a big difference between self-esteem and self-compassion. I read an article so I'm an expert. Which raises my self-esteem. Unless I admit I'm only human and could be wrong, which is a real drag to my self-esteem but boosts my self-compassion.

I know what I'm talking about.

To simplify, self-esteem is often defined as how we feel in relation to others, and self-compassion as how we feel in relation to ourselves. I learned this as I prepared for a meeting with a number of my Wisdom Divas—Linda, Alison, Catherine, and Robin. Our women's group explores exciting topics that most people would run from because they already think they have enough self-esteem and self-compassion.

But we're not those people. We like to look deep into topics that help us become self-actualized, which is a whole different kind of self-awareness than selfish self-interest. Please take notes.

This is how we work: Someone picks an issue to explore, then we Google it or watch a TED Talk or read a book or visit a related environment. Then we share our observations over food, which is the only way we can stomach them.

Originally, we swore off any kind of food or drink, starving ourselves into wisdom. That lasted one meeting because, as people everywhere know, an idea without a corn chip will never go down unless you add a little self-zer. I mean seltzer. *Sorry!*

After years of doing this self-analysis, you'd think we'd be self-contained by now. But we're not that self-reliant. We seem to need each other to become self-confident because you know how the self is—way too self-conscious to see itself.

We need helpers, not that we listen to them.

But back to self-compassion, which could also be defined as self-acceptance, although that's sort of a subset of the broader topic. Don't get confused. We all agree we're not that great at self-love, specifically during self-critical times, which happen more than self-dom. I mean, seldom.

Back to the topic ...

Experts, that self-satisfied bunch, claim self-compassion is a key to self-esteem. It helps us feel better about ourselves which makes us seem better in comparison to other people who could care less because they're way too self-absorbed. Not that we are.

Beware. Too much focus on self-esteem can make you narcissistic, while too little can make you a lazy bum. Meantime, too much focus on self-compassion can make you a lazy bum, while too little can make you a miserable person.

Got it?

Obviously, it doesn't take Carl Jung to realize the goal is to fall somewhere in the middle, which many of us do naturally, meaning all this research—*a full ten minutes!*—may have been wasted since no matter how many self-compassion exercises a person does to change, they don't always self-stick. Exercises like talking to yourself kindly or holding your hand over your heart and saying, "I'm good enough just the way I am." Things that appear so right on paper but somehow fall prey to self-sabotage.

So much to self-reflect on! But oops, the food is gone.

Let's end with this: To raise your self-esteem, do the best you can at what you do. To raise your self-compassion, treat yourself like your own best friend—unless you don't like your friends, which, I'll note, is quite self-destructive.

That can be another topic.

But before we depart, let's take a selfie.

Layer Six:
Loving

The most open-hearted poses in yoga are backbends. They give you courage, strength, confidence, a sense of exhilaration. Meaning, they give you an extra dose of energy or *prana* to get out of the way of your small, clinging ego—*ahamkara* in yoga—so you can love the people you love, and why not more of them?

In fact, why not, on occasion, the whole wide world?

For example, *urdhva dhanurasana*, upward bow, a backbend that rises from the floor and takes your head upside down. You lie down, plant your hands and feet, raise your hips, straighten your arms and legs. Then, you LIFT! Your head and tail ultimately go in two opposite directions.

It's just like real life, when you try not to use the wrong end of your intelligence.

Whenever possible.

In backbends, instead of closing in on yourself by rounding your shoulders and sucking in your chest, you roll your shoulders back, raise your sternum up, and take a full, deep inhalation, filling your lungs and brain with fresh light and clarity, your chest expanding like available arms.

You are spacious and exhilarated, creating the ideal conditions to be more open to the people you love and to accept the people you don't, and when necessary, to throw up your hands and revel in the way things are. And if you still can't do any of those things, you sit down and write about it—scribble any which way you can on any tiny scrap of paper to clear your brain—before you bite off a beloved's head.

A married woman walks into a bar

I took my wedding band off at a bar. Okay, fine, I admit it. But it had nothing to do with what I had in mind. I swear.

It was all for my friend who was celebrating one of those birthdays that ends in a five or a zero. A birthday that could send you crying on your pillow for a night or a year if you don't attack it just right. She's single, and the best way to attract the perfect pick-me-up to a disheartening milestone, I figured, was to create an atmosphere of alluring, seductive, black widow singleness around her so she could snare a great guy in her web.

I feared a married woman in the vicinity might send the wrong dull message.

So, for the first time in decades, while at a bar at the New Jersey shore, I slipped off my white gold band and placed it on the other hand. It felt weird and naked and risky and horribly dangerous. In other words, it felt great.

I knew Ray wouldn't know because he happened to be working overseas, which sounds sort of convenient if I had my mind in the gutter. Which I didn't. But he wouldn't find out. Unless, come to think of it, he saw this.

"Hi, honey," I said out loud. "Thinking of you. How's the weather in France, anyway?"

If I got in trouble, I'd blame it all on my friend Noelle.

In addition to being from exotic New Zealand, Noelle went to finishing school and says things like "Sit up straight" and "That's not ladylike." But this was a big birthday so filled with her usual poise and great manners, she leapt across our hotel lobby, took the concierge by the collar, and demanded she find us "two hot men for the night."

The words came out of her mouth so unexpectedly and with such vehemence, I could do nothing but helplessly follow along. The concierge looked at us like we wouldn't know hot men from hot oatmeal. Insulted, I stood my ground—for birthday solidarity only—and announced respectfully, "Thank you very much but we can find our own babe magnets."

What else could I do, Your Honor, ruin my friend's big night out?

Have you ever noticed that married women find all sorts of men attractive so long as they're attractive for someone else? I always tell my single friends, "You can overlook the belly and the crusty nails and maybe a little bit of a smell, but we can certainly work on the clothes, can't we?"

But faced with the possibility one of these guys could be my guy for the night, they didn't look so good. *I'm serious, honey, they looked awful!*

Once, when Noelle and I were younger, a bartender interceded for some patrons who wanted to know if we came there often. We laughed so hard we made ourselves grossly unattractive half spitting our wine and falling off our bar stools. No one ever came over.

We decided this night would be different, even if I happened to get married in between.

"Sleep tight, honey!"

What happened next was as mysterious to me as how to find a good husband. When my ring came off, suddenly I remembered what an awful flirt I am. It all came flooding back, like swimming or riding a bike. Who knew it was like a God-given instinct?

So who did we meet at the Jersey shore that night? A thirty-eight-year-old self-proclaimed "people person" who kept referring to his dirty, rotten, cheating ex-girl-friend as "pretty girl," and believe me he didn't say this in a nice voice. And a seventy-five-year-old sailor searching for a "young, in-shape woman" ready to crew with him to Florida, all cozy in a small boat for weeks, even though they wouldn't know each other from a mainsail or a jib.

In my usual married state, I would have thought the birthday girl should snag both of them. (Where was she, anyway, was I supposed to be watching her?) But in my single condition, I somehow recognized them for exactly what they were: the reason a woman ever agrees to get married and stay out of the bars in the first place.

Girlfriend versus wife

There's a big difference between a woman acting like a girlfriend as opposed to a wife. That's what a man on a motorcycle told me. He and his longtime "bride" were on a Honda Gold Wing plowing through 2,500 miles of supposedly fun summer vacation.

Despite being sandwiched between him and the bike like a piece of Velveeta, despite being a dumpster for flying debris, despite being jerked and jumbled like gravel, he said her real strength was "she acts like my girlfriend, not like my wife."

She smiled. You know that smile—very un-girlfriendy, very wifey—that says, "When I get you alone, I'm gonna show you the two words 'girl' and 'friend' don't always go together."

And yet it got me thinking. What were some of those so-called girlfriend qualities?

✓ You're mostly happy to see him.
✓ You care how you look.

✓ You smell good.
✓ You occasionally cook a gourmet meal.
✓ You laugh at his lousy jokes.
✓ You pay attention to his boring stories.
✓ You don't force him to get a colonoscopy.

The way I figure it, none of these things even applies on the back of a motorcycle. Except the last. Because if you've ridden papoose for any length of time, which I have, you wonder if you need a colonoscopy. You don't feel good, you don't look good unless you're all suited up and don't look like you, which he might like, and you do nothing but sit. You sit, and you sit, and you sit.

Which eventually makes you think about that colonoscopy.

I asked her if she ever drove the thing. She said "No," though many women do of course. They sit and they drive, which is a whole lot better than just sitting. Any activity you add to sitting is an improvement, even if it's just pulling out the nail file, which you can't do on the back of a bike without it flying away.

You also can't laugh at his jokes because you can't hear them, although he may tell them anyway. You can't listen to his monotonous stories after a long day, because by the time you arrive at your destination, with all that engine noise, you're functionally deaf.

You're never happy to see him because you can't see him since you're behind him. You can't cook because it's hard to drag food around when your vehicle is a tin can itself.

And as far as smelling fresh and clean is concerned, you smell like road pizza.

On the back of a bike, I can't see how acting like a girlfriend is much help at all.

But acting like a wife? If your lips still worked after a long day of flapping in the wind, you could ask if he'd added oil or checked the tires and the gas. You could make sure he eats his vegetables so the antioxidants counteract the pollution from breathing car exhaust. You could make sure he exercises to keep his heart pumping and his limbs moving so he doesn't fall when he tries to extract himself from the bike. All helpful things a wife would do, while a girlfriend primps.

Yet after meeting this tough guy with his twig-infested beard and hardworking beer belly, I'd advise his mate, if she wants to get home alive, to keep her chest snuggled against his leather-clad back, but not "have his back" like a wife would.

And if he complains—you're not acting sexy enough, you don't adore me enough—bat your eyes and as soon as you can, make that dreaded "down there" doctor appointment he's been putting off for years. He'll never suspect a thing with those goggles covering your sweet, pretty face.

Mr. Romance saves the day

"If you diss me in your column, I'll kill you."

That's how a pre-anniversary week started at my house, and I wonder how many of you also find your significant other, maybe not the most extravagant sentimentalist, setting the stage for a showdown on a critical day of love.

Have no fear. Mr. Romance comes to the rescue. Now all you must do is get your mate to read this.

Let's get right down to it because this could be an emergency.

Mr. Romance is every man's nightmare. While your average Joe goes to Trader Joe's for a cuppa joe on anniversary morning, plus a bouquet of wilting blossoms, this particular Joe, his real name, plots to "best himself."

Mr. Romance throws subtlety to the wind.

For example, in the past he has:

- Stormed his wife's fourth grade classroom in a tux, climbed on her desk, and presented flowers while the kids stomped and cheered.

- Convinced a neighbor-turned-online-minister to remarry them in their living room.
- Kidnapped "the woman of his dreams" from her chiropractic appointment, blindfolded her, and whisked her to a horse and carriage ride.
- Lined a path to their bathtub with rose petals, a candlelit bubble bath waiting.
- Turned their living room into *Café de l'Amour*, complete with sparkly lights, a roaring fire, French music, and lobster.

The kind of fawning guys hate him for. In other words, if I use his last name, a hitman could follow.

And yet ...

Whenever the subject arises, his guy friends lean in. They want Joe's top tips for sending their mates swooning for all sorts of reasons. They, too, want to be Joe Smooth instead of Joe Schmo.

What does Joe know?

I called him to ask, ready to receive decades of wisdom and perhaps hidden obsessions about lovemaking rituals borrowed from his fellow animals: drinking blood, strutting displays, chest puffing, regurgitating food, cannibalism.

I shouldn't give Joe any new ideas.

And I called because I know his friends secretly wish he'd give a crash course in Romance 101. And I called because I know he's onto something. His wife says she feels so precious to him, feels like Cinderella instead of the Elayne that she is. That's a hard fairy tale to follow.

Me: So are you ever going to give a course?

Joe: Well, I've already thought of a name. I'll call it, "If I have to tell you what I want, why bother?"

Me: Ah, I couldn't agree more. I hate it when I'm asked what I want. Even if I get it, I hardly care anymore.

Joe: That's the point. To be truly romantic, you need to pull a rabbit out of a hat. And you can't ask your mate to go find the rabbit and the hat.

Me: So romance is magic?

Joe: I'd say romance is artistry. It's not a formula you can write about in a book or teach. You need to feel it, you need to invent it, you need to believe in it. You can't make copies of it. It's an original piece of art. It should be new each time.

Me: But if a guy's not Romeo, how can he keep the peace? What's your advice for buffoons who muddle through this anniversary charade like it's another Monday at work?

Joe: Okay, you forced me. Here goes one, two, three:

1. Know your person. Not everyone wants to be led upstairs for a risqué date with whipped cream and strawberries.
2. Romance is not a minute or an hour or a day thing. You need to put thoughtfulness into every moment.
3. Make whatever you create enjoyable for both of you. Otherwise, you won't feel a bang for your buck.

Me: But how about the time you lined your bedroom with moldy, smelly, pointy bales of hay and asked Cinderella to have a nice romp in it. She almost stabbed you with a pitchfork.

Joe: *C'est la vie* at *Café de l'Amour.*

Forks and spoons
make me swoon

Living with another person is about as easy as, well, living with yourself. Although when it comes to yourself, at least the odd quirks and assorted annoyances are to be expected.

With other people, however, it can be a bit of a surprise or even a shock to learn they don't do everything the way you do, won't do everything the way you do, don't think it's a good idea to do everything the way you do. And when you ask why, it's one flimsy excuse after another just piled on.

"Why don't you fold the towels in squares, not rectangles?" you might ask. "Who taught you to do it that way?"

As the philosopher Jean-Paul Sartre said decades ago, "Hell is other people."

Certainly, not you.

What kind of music at what volume is acceptable? At what point does clean become dirty? Do toothbrushes belong in a cabinet or on a counter? How does one properly cut a mango? These are the questions that plague many mates.

Those poorly raised, badly misinformed, just-plain-wrong people can make you become a solitary lone wolf, a hermit in sync only with the rising and setting of the sun. Roommates can make you want to howl—too lazy, too always on their phones, too disheveled, too loud, too dumb.

Certainly, not you.

Ray once said, "At least when you die, they'll say you had a clean, organized house." Then he cackled to taunt me for wanting a simple thing like all the same foods on the same shelf in the refrigerator.

Why separate a dairy or antioxidant family for no good reason?

No, I wasn't always this way.

When I was young, living at home, my room was a hazardous waste site, a landfill, a repository of all things crumpled and crusty. I had a secret ashtray under the bed, piles of scorned clothes dumped in corners, half-eaten Almond Joys sticking inside my night table. At any given time, I had an album, a radio, a hair dryer, a princess phone, a cheese melt, and a face steamer all going at once, while I studied.

It was all those quiet, organized types like Mom who made me cackle. Yes, hell was other people.

Yet as soon as I had my first apartment, the slob vanished like a teenager when it's time to do the dishes. I became a clean freak, a Comet and Windex junkie, a no-smoking-allowed fanatic, the one who dictated to everyone how they should make their beds and scrub their tubs. I taught one roommate how to spritz a mirror, another how to spread the fringe on a carpet.

See, Mom, I changed. Grew up, I guess, plain and simple. The person I live with today might say I went backward.

"Does it really matter?" Ray asked when I traded a big spoon for a little one as I embarked on a bowl of hot soup. "I don't like a big spoon," I grunted as I marched to the drawer for a replacement. "Too much slurping."

"Yes, yes," he grumbled, "and you eat dinner with a big fork, not a little one.

"And you prefer two napkins, one on your lap and one on the table, and you want the heat turned up because you like to strip down when you eat. And you want salad dressing on the side and let's turn down the lights because bright lights mess with melatonin production at night and please no ice in my water, you know it gives me a headache, and really who wants to listen to the news while eating, it's so bad for digestion."

"Wow," I said, beaming. "I think you've finally got it."

"Now sit down," he replied. "Dinner is served. It's your favorite: food you don't have to cook yourself."

Heaven is other people, too.

The male Spanx experiment

I was so surprised to see Spanx in the men's department at Nordstrom, I thought I would accidentally release the permanent suck from wearing Spanx to tidy up my own saggy middle.

"Is this a joke?" I blurted, as images of beer bellies and love handles morphed into superheroes shaped like a V. "Are guys buying these?"

"Spanx is a billion-dollar industry," a trim and tidy salesman explained. Maybe a billion for women, I thought, but for bulging gents with a Captain America fetish, a few pennies dribbled here and there. Real men don't give a damn.

"Men are wearing eye shadow too," he whispered, trying not to embarrass me for being so out of touch. Then he finished his hard-sell pitch: "Not just gay men, straight men."

Really?

With a convenient straight man at home, I decided to put this "expect more from your undershirt" hogwash to the test. If my straight man agreed to wear Spanx, nicknamed Manx for men, I'd march back in there and eat my shorts—I mean my Spanx—even the super-duper shapers with *buttlets* for added junk in the trunk.

I'd spent years trying to get the guy at home to put moisturizer on his dry skin, sunscreen on his red skin, whiten his teeth, use hair gel, wear skinny European suits, and lose the un-Spanx-ness that has settled around his waist. He won't even let me use his pocket for gooey lipstick so I don't have to carry a purse, while he refuses to use a man bag.

Would this kind of guy wear Manx?

Manx undershirts come in two helpful shapes, one with sleeves and one without. Since my token straight man gets hot wearing socks, I chose the hardcore Level 3 tank that firms the chest, narrows the waist, flattens the stomach, improves posture, and most critically, is made of breathable cotton.

If the tank can breathe, maybe Ray won't notice he can't.

There was one reason I thought this would work. In the past week, he had tried on seventeen wetsuits because he was jealous I have one. Me looking more buff than he does rubs his ego like tight clothes give him a rash. For days he'd been modeling these suits, primping and flexing, looking like Lloyd Bridges in that classic *Sea Hunt* show.

Trusting my *thin-stincts*, a Spanx-y term, I tried my luck getting him into Manx.

"So Spanx feels like a wetsuit," he uttered, playing right into my hands. The fact you wear one underwater avoiding sharks and the other in a bar sipping cocktails *did not* imme-diately occur to him.

It *did* occur to him that he could look five pounds thin-ner so I'd stop nagging him, plus he'd get a layer of warmth should he flex his pecs in Iceland. He even called the experiment "our little spank-a-thon."

With the strength of a weightlifter and the perseverance of an endurance athlete, he pulled the skintight Manx over his head, and lo and behold, I saw the V at his waist and fully expected an H on his chest: H for hunk.

"You look slim and trim whether or not you hit the gym," I mewed, adding a little more Spanx verbiage.

Then he tried to get it off. I mean really, really tried.

First it was fun: "Did this come with insurance because I might hurt myself," he said, laughing. Then this: "I can curl forty-five pounds in each hand, but I can't pull this over my head." Then this: "If I tear a rotator cuff, I'll sue their *buttlets*." And finally, this: "Get me the scissors, I swear, get me the scissors!"

The results of the test? The "fit was a hit" but the "hunk flunked."

Maybe Spanx should sell wetsuits. For that, I believe he would suffer.

A foxy new year

It sounded like this at my house before the big night arrived:

"I want to go," I said to Ray, "no matter how young we aren't." I was scanning the Internet for pictures of the Caribbean's hottest New Year's Eve party at Foxy's on the island of Jost Van Dyke in the British Virgin Islands. We would be on St. John, a mere island away.

"It says here there's copious drinking, sparkly bikinis, and a lack of shirts for men," I announced, looking at a website.

"You're kiddin' me," he replied.

"This says it's not unusual for revelers to stay overnight on the beach, and quite common, in fact, to see tangles of bodies, er, recuperating together from the festivities."

"So we have to tangle?"

"We could get a ferry back to St. John at 2 a.m. but it could take hours to get through customs. Jost is British and St. John is American," I explained. "They're mother and child but they have serious problems communicating."

"We could spend hours waiting in line?"

"There'll be drunks singing 'Auld Lang Syne' way past

midnight," I merrily responded, "and they'll be hugging and kissing us as if we were new best friends."

"I thought you hated germs."

"Our immune systems will be all pumped up from competing for a first-come, first-served BBQ with hundreds of sweaty, grinding twenty-somethings pawing their way through the spicy ribs."

"Food poisoning?"

"No worries," I joyfully declared. "We'll kill anything by slapping down the Sly Fox, the Dread Fox, the Wreck on the Rocks, and all the other deadly rum drinks."

"We'll be drinking with hundreds of kids with no parental guidance?"

"There'll be yacht people there, too, who arrive in their dinghies," I added. "They pin their keys to whatever body part has clothes on or they'll never find them again."

"We don't have a yacht."

"We could pay 135 dollars each to go ten miles on a packed ferry," I countered, "or buy a twenty-foot runabout we could use every time we go."

"We're buying a boat?"

"If we don't, there'll be no room to sit once we get there. Everyone is elbow to elbow or shoulder to shoulder; they can't raise their arms."

"I don't see anyone over thirty in that group," he replied, pointing to my computer screen.

"That woman there is at least thirty-five," I firmly insisted. "I can tell by the stretch marks."

"I thought that was a permanent crease from being crushed by the crowd."

"You're so negative," I shouted. "We're going!"

"You'll have to drag along your aspirin and acid reflux meds," he cautioned, "and you'll never find a bathroom, let alone water. And did you forget you can't handle your liquor?"

"We'll be dancing our asses off," I yelled. "Who cares about anything else?"

"You'll have to wear your knee wrap in case you slip."

"That's a terrible look. I'll be in a bikini!"

"Is that a joke?"

"Was *that* a joke?"

"Look, if that's what you want, I'll go," he agreed. "It's been a long time since I've danced bare-chested and woken up with sand in my hair and a new babe in my arms."

"Bare-chested? You're kiddin' me."

"Who cares if we can't get back?" he said, grinning. "We could spend the whole next day comatose and wandering, half naked with a hangover, the last and oldest people to leave Foxy's. We'll show 'em! I'm sure we'll get back to St. John somehow, someday, so we don't miss our flight home."

Hmmm … I pondered.

Hmmm … he pondered.

"I know," I muttered. "What if we ferry over to Foxy's during the day, just to say we've been there, done that—get the feel of the debauchery before it actually debauches—then hop back on a boat before things go ballistic?"

"Then," he added, "what if we splurge on a scandalously high-priced dinner of pathetically small portions overlooking the sea, then go to bed at some reasonable hour with the same person in our arms. We'll even wear funny hats."

Hmmm ... we both pondered.

Mission accomplished!

Old boyfriends never die

When I saw an old boyfriend at a party, I expected him to still look eighteen. First, I heard someone call his name and saw a finger point in his direction. Then I saw the back of his head. He still had a full head of hair, a good sign. Then I saw the back of his black cashmere coat. Fashionable, expensive. Maybe he'd made it big.

I waited with such anticipation I thought Ray would slap me upside the head. In that split second of expectation, I obviously looked like the blushing combination of perky and pathetically hooked that got me into trouble when I fell for someone. I was wearing an ear-to-ear smile I couldn't wipe off.

Then he turned, achingly slowly, oblivious to the fact a former love stood behind him, waiting to be rediscovered.

And so began my latest adventure as the ex-boyfriend magnet.

Since the Internet, I've attracted ex-boyfriends like the Swiffer picks up dust.

Maybe they think I'll save them from the dustbin of old age by remembering how they strutted in college or triumphed at their first lousy jobs or survived the miserable angst of their twenties and thirties, back when they were still so darn cute.

There was Mr. Fix It who built me furniture, the Furniture Schlepper who carried it from apartment to apartment, the Car Guy with his new and maybe stolen wheels, the White Knight with his white suit and white motorcycle who drove up a full set of steps to fetch me, the Alcoholic Rock Climber who drank from a flask while I dangled below. I've mixed up details here because some of them were big losers with a capital L and I don't want stalkers with a capital S.

Maybe I didn't always choose so well.

I had one boyfriend, the Kisser, who gave me my first smooch then told everyone. He became a federal agent, but I bet he still kisses and tells.

Another surfaced as a radical; I call him the Unabomber. I remember he hated to talk, but now he writes long philosophical emails about the past. I hope he's in therapy.

In my backward mind, let's call it my rigid reptilian brain, each one of these guys is frozen in time, still playing guitar or shooting baskets or being a filthy, dirty, delusional bum on his way to becoming a doctor, lawyer, or starving artist. In my mind, none of them has changed.

Why should they? Aren't ex-boyfriends props in your personal history of conquest and popularity, heartbreak and revenge? Characters for outlandish stories about the disasters of dating, the hordes that wined and dined you, the guys who wanted to crown you wife, princess, queen, or the guys who were the biggest creeps who could beat all other creeps any day of the week.

Them, I'd like to hunt down and stalk.

For me, old boyfriends come in five different packages. The rare ones you become friends with, the ones you hear titillating tidbits about that make you feel either superior or second-rate, the ones who dig you up no matter what, the ones you're dying to find but can't locate in any Internet nook and cranny, and the ones who suddenly pop up for no reason while you're going about your business.

Like this guy turning achingly slowly in my direction. Turning, turning, turning as I held my breath to see what became of Frenchy, a sweetheart from college. Let's just say I call him that because we took language class together. The rest I can't discuss in public.

So there he was, face-to-face, with grown-up me. Let's make that eighteen-year-old me, because he'd clearly paid the price for not snapping me up when he had the chance. The more he turned, the younger I got.

But I'll never kiss and tell any more than that. To me, he's as wonderful as when we stared at each other across the bright lights and metal desks and whispered what I'd like to say to each one of these guys: "*Je t'adore* 'til the end of time."

For the old stories that still make me blush, I adore you.

A tale of revenge

We had simultaneously read the best revenge story of all time, *The Count of Monte Cristo*, so I feared Ray would plot his own kind of revenge when he learned I hit his newish car in the driveway. Immediately, I ran to the seafood market and grabbed an Alaskan king crab leg, nearly sixty bucks a pound. Crab legs totally disturb me and make me sad, but not Ray. And since I was about to reveal that while he was out pedaling his two-wheeler in his short bike pants, I hit his fancy four-wheeled Volvo because—well—I forgot to look behind me, I thought I'd better be ready with a coveted offering when I got on my knees and begged for mercy.

The dent was only minor, the scratch superficial, but I knew he'd slap one hand on his forehead, his eyes would bulge, and his breath would get loud and short. Then he'd walk with giant, aching, theatrical strides to the scene of the event.

I shuddered and pondered. *Should I grab the smelling salts?*

The Count of Monte Cristo is one of a handful of long books that made a pandemic appearance at our house after

I announced it was time we tackle some of the great literature we always said we would read. We're not getting any younger, I moaned. It's now or never. Yet I'm aware golden oldies like this can have a downside. They can inspire us to plot destruction on others, like me, who plain screw up.

In the classic story, slow, methodical, and sweet revenge is taken on those who sent the Count to prison on false charges. We learned about endless ways a victim can make his culprits desperately miserable if they have years of patience and an amount of cash that would make Jeff Bezos and Bill Gates look poor.

Ray certainly didn't fall into that category, but I thought the book may have given him ideas I couldn't predict, like pouring water on my car seat or changing the preset radio stations.

The Count of Monte Cristo wasn't the only vintage choice during that first long pandemic winter. We also read *War and Peace* and learned that even at the worst of times, like bashing into your mate's car, peace can eventually reign again. I could only hope.

And we both finally read *Crime and Punishment*, again revealing a timeless message that swiftly struck me to the core: somehow, in some way, you will pay.

After asking Ray to close his eyes because I had two surprises, one a treat and one a confession, and after watching him stride slow motion to the car, I had to endure all sorts of head shaking, mainly because the dent was minor. If it wasn't—like the dent I suddenly recalled he planted on my car several years back—the response would have unleashed far more venom.

And just like that, that earlier event in reverse flashed before my eyes. Maybe this was, after all, my own long-awaited revenge. *Aha!*

In that past affair, Ray had rushed off to work after crushing my side door, never confessing until I called him to report an unidentified hit-and-run at our house. No offering on bended knees did I receive. No flowers, nothing.

Sweet revenge, I thought, smiling at his scowl. *Gotcha!* The Count would be proud.

Except, the Count would have been disappointed to learn that after a wash and wax, the Volvo didn't look half bad, while my own car, the poor Honda that did the dirty work, looked worse.

Got me! Again!

Disasters, certainly, are aplenty, and of course none of this adds up to the calamitous crises in these iconic books. Still, next time we want to cozy up together and read a tale, just in case, I think I'll suggest something light, humorous, loving, and refreshingly forgiving.

Moby Dick?

Love costs $8.99

If one Valentine's Day card doesn't say it all—not the mushy one or the funny one or the singing one or the sexy one—you could get in serious trouble.

Me: This is the card you got me?

Him: I thought it was funny.

Me: How about the one that says in all the world, you're the only one made just for me?

Him: That one costs more.

Me: Good choice.

Even if you do get it right, when you go to your Hallmark store, you have the sense of being taken for a ride and it's not to the chapel of love.

For example, "I love the way we text." If you love it so much, why not text? Why pay $8.99 for a card as hi-tech as washing clothes on a rough stone or cooking the raw flesh of a buffalo over an open flame?

And we feel guilty, right, about not coming up with our own sentiments but being a parasite to others so much better at the most important key to a good relationship, communication.

Well, take a page from Romeo and Juliet at my house. It doesn't have to end so badly.

Me: Are you ready for our annual Valentine's Day excursion?

Him: I suddenly feel very tired.

Me: Let's get it over with.

Years ago, after buying lame cards that said something but not everything, or others that said something we could have said ourselves, and still more that said something then ended up in a keepsake box never to be reopened, Ray and I decided to go to Hallmark together and cheat.

Meaning, we stand before rows of cards dripping in roses, cute animals, giant hearts, glitter, sequins, and the occasional rude body gesture designed to indicate the great comfort of a longtime love, and we explore. Then I pick a card I coulda, woulda, shoulda bought for one penny short of six or eight or ten dollars, and I hand it over. He gets his smirk or blush or giggle, and it goes back on the shelf. Then it's his turn.

This goes on until one of us gets sick of fawning and swooning, and we call it a holiday.

In between, we laugh like idiots, wondering if the store clerks have caught on. We're manhandling the merchandise with no intention of buying, our sticky hands—we always start with some low-brow lunch—perhaps providing the evidence of our subterfuge.

Yet it's romantic in that we're-in-this-dumb-thing-together kind of way. Out loud he reads, "You are hot pink in a sea of beige," and bats his eyes like hummingbird wings. I tingle.

"What a man you are," I say next, adoringly, or at least someone better than me said that.

He counters, "I love the sh*t outta you." Yes, a real card.

And I retort, "Are you a campfire? 'Cause you are hot and I want s'more."

He groans and adds, "Our love is bigger and stronger than most couples and I'm proud of that."

Yeah, right.

I punt with, "I love everything about you. Except those things we've already discussed."

Now we're getting closer to home.

Dusted in sticky red shimmer, I know we're near the end when Ray gets philosophical and says something like, "If you have to get a serious card, you should just get a divorce. A funny card is the only thing that makes sense in a longtime marriage."

Then we fall on the floor clutching our bellies—*They're on to us now*—and tumble out of the store drunk with the final convulsions of the yearly Valentine's Day jaunt.

We take the money we didn't spend and buy ourselves a gift we don't need—wine glasses, coffee mugs, a candle for the bedroom—something maybe we'll use. Maybe.

In the end we didn't save a dime, but we imagine we saved a tree.

And this we call love, too.

Good riddance, Luddite

When you spend a lot of time with your house-mates, like during a deep snowy winter or a pandemic, there comes a time when two of you, or all of you, simply don't agree.

In which case, a well-placed word could go a long way. It may go a long way in the wrong direction, however, and it may have legs that follow you for quite an annoying time. Your housemates may not like what you called them.

This word, for example: Luddite.

Because Ray and I were having a so-called discussion, and I was accusing him of being narrow-minded and back-ward, and he was accusing me of being a nag, I called him this old-fashioned word. Which led him to look up the defi-nition and discover the Luddite in the house is me, because it means the kind of person who would rather write in pen and ink than fire up the computer. A Luddite is someone who shuns modern technology, named after English work-ers who did just that.

I was using it all wrong. He doesn't shun technology; he shuns plain common sense.

He followed this remark by calling me a "doofus and goofus." I pointed out this is a meathead expression used by people who are too lazy to search for more appropriate and cutting words. They're namby-pamby terms like half-wit and yo-yo, I said—so infantile—to which, in the maturity gained from being stuck with him in the house, I called him a Neanderthal.

I did this because I read that people of European descent still have two percent Neanderthal DNA, which, as a Luddite, I claimed he uses on a regular basis to show he's more valuable than me because he can do something fancy like sharpen a large knife. I informed him this is an obsolete hunter-gatherer activity and, anyway, at this stage of our togetherness we should have removed all the cleavers from the house.

Which made him call me a bore, defined as a dull and tiresome person who provides nothing interesting to say.

Blah, blah, blah, babble, babble, babble, was all I could add in response.

Most of the time though, during the pandemic winters, we kept things copasetic.

But not always. Or sometimes. Or hardly.

Certainly not, I pointed out, when he acted like an ordinary clod, which I could finally say when spring arrived and I could get out of the house. After we deconstructed the topic of how well we got along with a newfound freedom we didn't dare display earlier when it was too risky because we were stuck.

Looking up the official definition of clod, I came across this sentence as an example and read it out loud: "You are an insensitive clod and I hope you fall and break your neck."

I pointed out that I didn't say that the dictionary did, so don't blame me.

He countered with "philistine," which he knew would get under my skin because I'm nothing like that old neighbor Phyllis who was quite a dolt, a stupid person. Philistine, he read on his phone as he shook his head, was another word I'd been using all wrong.

"In the fields of philosophy and aesthetics," he read, "the derogatory term philistinism describes the manners, habits, and character of a person whose anti-intellectual social attitude undervalues and despises art and beauty, spirituality and intellect."

"Stop talking about yourself," I said. "It's rude, egotistical, and in my opinion, sickening."

To which he said, "Maybe-I-am-but-what-about-you?" Then he stuck out his tongue and wiggled his fingers with his thumbs in his ears as I turned away to leave the house.

And I went, I finally went. I left the house free and easy, good riddance, chump.

But before I drove off, I asked what kind of takeout I should pick up for dinner.

Over the moon together

I have a guy who needs convincing.

Him: No, no way, nope.

Me: Oh, come on. We'll get up at 4 a.m., nearly sunrise in some parts of the world. We'll throw our coats over our pajamas and take a tiny ride. I'll drive.

Him: We don't wear pajamas.

Me: I'll cover up this old ratty nightgown and you can throw on some sweatpants. *Eazy peezy. Pleazy?*

Him: Absolutely not.

Me: It could affect you for the rest of your life you know. People go through all kinds of changes when they do this kind of thing.

Him: I'm already changed enough. Enough! You and your ideas. I'm going to bed.

Me: If that's all you want out of life, fine with me. *Humph.*

Him: That's all I want. You should be used to it by now. *Humph.*

I pulled down the blackout shades, climbed into the

cozy bed with a heated mattress cover, and considered setting the alarm for 4 a.m. *Really?* Did I need to jump into the winter night alone, inch my car out of the clunky garage, swerve into blackness with all sorts of nighttime animals like deer, fox, maybe a mountain lion, who knows? It would be an obstacle course to get where I was going.

Which, by the way, was to the moon.

So I didn't set the alarm. Maybe I'm already changed enough, too.

At 4, my body knew better. I popped up.

Aren't there all sorts of things you want that your partner doesn't? He skis; I don't anymore. I do yoga and meditate; he doesn't. He watches grade B superhero movies; I can't understand why. I go from museum to museum, happy, tired; his back aches after one.

He could live on rice; I want potatoes. A good meal to him has few vegetables; broccoli is my secret weapon. His coffee has milk and sugar; my green tea is naked. A good day to him is quiet and slow; to me, it's busy and full. When we travel, he wants to stay in one place and explore from there. I want to move, move, move.

But the moon? Who can't agree on that?

At 4, as I grabbed my coat—stomping my feet and slamming doors in case someone, somewhere wanted to join me—I hesitated. I walked outside, shivered, doubted I'd go anywhere, and got a surprise.

The full moon was shining in the backyard, a full-on view of the lunar eclipse underway right there at home.

Scarcely the need to get out of bed. No drive to a distant lookout, no scary animals.

I took off my coat, settled back upstairs near a bedroom window—dragging a chair, stomping into position—because I know how this goes.

Him, drowsy: What's happening?

Me: It's the lunar eclipse right outside our window. Go back to bed. So sorry if I woke you. Sooo, sooo sorry. I was trying to be sooo quiet. *Wink, wink.*

Him, perking up: Did you grab the binoculars? Go get the binoculars. Is this really the best view? Did you look from my office window? How much more time do we have? I heard it's supposed to get dark red. Will we see it until the end, or will it hide behind the trees?

With the moon and stars as my witness, I turned to look at him as he climbed out of bed, dragged a chair, and sat next to me.

I said nothing. Not what-are-you-kidding-me or are-you-totally-nuts? I already knew the game at our house. It goes like this: he says no then yes, and I say yes then no.

He also typically points a finger in my direction: "Don't wear me down. You know how you wear me down. Don't do it."

Little ole' me?

On the other hand, I'm ready to jump into anything, get myself into trouble, then say, "Why didn't you warn me? You never warn me. You know how I am."

And I know how he is.

Sitting together, passing the binoculars between us, watching the moon turn deep red, I gazed upward and thanked the heavens for saving me from scary lions and saving him from having to carry his lazy butt outside.

We watched as the moon changed us—reminded us we're not the center of the universe, just tiny players in a vast mystery, with the big important things in life out of our control.

Like our mates, for example.

Wink, wink, wink.

Real men do salsa

S alsa isn't one of those dances you do with a bunch of tipsy girlfriends while a group of comatose guys look on. And it's not one of those dances where girls do all the wiggling and men lend a helping hand. The guys in front of me were into every twist and turn.

"They're not being forced by the women at all," I shouted. "Just look at them!"

I knew I was gushing, but, but, but ...

This is how I was talking to Ray as we stood plastered against a wall in a salsa club in Havana. We were at *Casa de la Musica* with a slew of young Cubans, old Cubans, a combustible mix of hips just short of dislocation, shoulders heaving, derrieres swinging, steam rising, and if I explain any more you will faint like from your first kiss.

"I can't believe what's going on here, Ray. Look, look, look!"

The couples were spinning so fast, we were afraid of being trapped like fruit in a blender. Ray is a willing dancer, but salsa, not so much. Me neither. We were hoping if we watched first, fueled by a sense of what happens in Cuba stays in Cuba, we'd have the guts to join in, because did I mention it was not just the women who were making a case for a Category 5 hurricane triggering a volcanic eruption, but the men, too.

Especially one guy, maybe six foot two and dressed in pure white, with deep black Rasta braids down his sharp, muscled back. He was smiling, he was rocking his rump, he was pulling his girl in close, their eyes were locked. A real cool dude. I saw Ray staring at him thinking maybe if this he-man can do it, maybe he, too, could loosen his joints, discover his Latin lover, and find his true macho mojo. His brain seemed to be sloshing in his head like giggling bottoms.

"Don't worry," I said. "These people were weaned on salsa. We come from the land that invented foxtrot. If we get in there, we'll embarrass ourselves, our families, our generation, our country. Even I don't think we can do it."

But I wanted to.

"Wait," I said. "No one here knows us, what harm can it do? Let's yank our hips out of their sockets, clean out the lard, and reinsert them with brand new parts while we still have the chance. We can't pass this up."

But we did.

We survived a good couple of hours near our wall, too scared to even sip our drinks for fear we'd topple over. There was too much aphrodisiac in the air.

We found ourselves later at a nightclub filled with tourists. They couldn't salsa, either. There was a teacher named Juan trying to change that. He was tight, cute, and vibrating like Jell-O in black silk. He drew me in, turned me, twirled me, jerked me close, whispered, "You're a good dancer." Ray ruined the moment, I mean, suddenly showed up.

"You must learn three basic steps before you do anything fancy," instructed Juan.

"This is not what I bargained for," droned Ray, noticing the whole room watching.

"Let 'em watch," I declared. "Real men do salsa."

"Quick-quick-slow," said Juan, teaching the basic one-two-three count for steps. "Salsa is explosive, let go, move those hips, quick-quick-slow."

"Bad salsa," he quickly moaned, pointing to Ray's feet.

"He doesn't really mean bad," I murmured. "It's just the language issue. Probably he means horrible, which sounds so much better in Spanish: *or-ee-blay*."

"Remember the dude in white," I added. "How cool was he?"

Something shifted—his macho mojo?—or maybe it was the rum. As the music swirled around us, Ray gathered his own seismic force. Bad salsa, for a fraction of a second—a barely perceptible moment—turned into good, hot, spicy salsa. Our eyes locked, and horrible turned into *or-ee-blay* turned into *Dude!* And the room fell away.

Layer Seven:
Knowing

At a certain stage in your evolution, you already know all the good, wise advice about how to be your best self. It's not about the information. You've heard it, you've read it, you've got it! It's about doing what you've learned, which is a whole different animal and not necessarily one you'd like to adopt.

Yet at some point, you realize you can't keep talking about it, analyzing and rationalizing and philosophizing about it, you need to put that well-earned knowledge into everyday practice in work, in the community, with friends, family, with the losers you meet, and most of all with yourself.

The hard part is here.

Yoga is designed to teach you—*tries to teach you*—to become a master of yourself. No small thing. That means getting inside your thoughts and behaviors, those sticky, crummy habits, and cleansing them before they set you on a worn-out path to somewhere you no longer want to go.

A good place to practice is s*avasana*, the corpse pose, which readies you not for that future reality—though it will come in handy—but for an unshakable trust in what you need and what you don't. How to think about a situation and how to act. How to make progress on achieving your goals. How to release your fears and finally let go.

How to believe you might truly be okay. Or okay enough.

You lie on your back, feet hip-width wide, arms away from your side body. Then you soften and spread, letting go of the tightness in your belly, your clenched palms, your stiff jaw, your crazy thoughts.

You let go, melt, release, making your breath light as a dragonfly landing on water, a blue morpho landing on a leaf, a whisp of fluff floating on the air—so that something new, welcome, unspoiled can come in.

Then you get up and carry that memory with you. *You try.*

America needs a nap

It's the middle of the day—maybe two o'clock, maybe four—and a light switch turns off in your head. Nervous, shaky, you start judging yourself. I'm all washed up, useless, lazy, stupid, soft, old.

You run for coffee, grab a breath of fresh air, get up and walk around, try to keep busy. Maybe you reach for dark chocolate—*it's an emergency*—thinking it will help your heart which may be failing since you feel so faint.

You close your eyes for a second. If only you could justify it, get away with it, let go of the guilt.

Admit it: You want to take a nap. Cuddle up and lay your bobbing head down to rest. *If only.* If only this wasn't America.

It's time to take our heads out of the sand and put them on a pillow. Napping in this country, as sleep-deprived zombies know, is often belittled as the slacker's Achilles heel, the dark cave of the unemployed sloth. Embarrassing. Sluggish. Weak.

But that's old school.

Today the nap is increasingly touted as the darling of intellectual and artistic types, doctors and scientists, business tycoons who say small sips of dead-to-the-world is a smart way to boost your focus, brighten your mood, and pump up those creative juices so you don't sit there staring into space researching topics like naps.

Caught me!

Besides, with all the constant attention on the balance of trade, a nap may be the best deal we have. Some of those siesta-loving countries are now going straight through the day, push, push, push, becoming more like us. Maybe it's time we take their afternoon lull in return, shift the balance of trade in our yawning direction.

Personally, I'm ready to concede I enjoy a brief climb down the deep well of oblivion. And why not? Why not join the long list of superior folks who had the guts to confess: Einstein, Churchill, Dali, DaVinci, to name a few historic nappers. Who doesn't want to be superior?

Did you know a full third of the adult population sneaks in a nap? That includes not just dull people but perky millennials who are more flexible about the nine to five. Better to grab a few winks than another cup of java or a jar of jellybeans.

Naps are pesticide-free, caffeine-free, sugar-free.

Old school: naps are for quitters. New school: naps are for doers who want to be at the top of their game.

A twenty-to-thirty-minute power snooze—on your back, in your car, under your desk—is the perfect amount of time to plug in the charger. Any complaints?

No doubt we've made great strides. Nap rooms have

been rolled out at top companies. Google and NASA have installed sleep pods to coddle brains that would rather be briefly wrapped in swaddling than banging down on a desk.

It can get bloody.

As you can tell, I'm building a case for a national nap proclamation. With perhaps unanimous voter support, I state the following:

In an age when things we never thought possible have been possible—gay marriage, legal marijuana, a reality show president—let's give up the illusion that a full day without a period of stone-cold unconsciousness is good for us.

It's free, it's available, it's quick, it's painless.

You don't need to smoke it, drink it, melt it under your tongue, pop it, vape it. You don't need to buy it. It costs nothing.

Name one other thing that feels so good, is so easy to do, and—as the research says—is so good for you. It soothes the heart, reduces stress, accidents, and dementia. Plus, it makes you nicer to live with, improves stamina, memory, cognitive ability, and helps you look younger.

You can even share it.

It's time, America. We have some problems going on here and we have no quick solutions. Here's one: maybe the whole country could use a nap.

Remember how your kids were when they didn't get one?

Cracking the friendship nut

" I miss everybody so much," moaned my then eighteen-year-old niece Molly, in college far from home on her semester abroad. "It's so hard to make new friends."

I needed to pull a rabbit out of a hat. You can't very well let a freshman sulk in a distant place with all the stress, fear, drama, drinking, and all-night partying that goes on. I was struggling for a nut of truth. One that would help things fall into place just fine.

"Let them borrow your clothes?" I volunteered, smirking.

We laughed. We hung up. I had failed.

Ralph Waldo Emerson popped into my head: "The only way to have a friend is to be one." I texted her back, feeling smart for a moment.

Then I pondered. *Is that old quote, like a dear friend from childhood, a keeper?*

And is it something we naturally know in our hearts, or do we need an education in this age of social media about what it means to be a friend and get one back?

Knowing

Pretty much everything we learn, or maybe need to learn, about being the kind of friend we want for ourselves fits under that Emerson banner. Accept the person's imperfections, listen without judgment, be there in their darkest hour, know when to be serious and when to be silly, be vulnerable, be their cheerleader, tell them when they have spinach in their teeth, watch their backs.

Was I supposed to remind her of those things?

Or perhaps practicalities were best. Find someone who shares your passions, make time for one-on-one intimacy not just selfies, join clubs, invite people to do things, smile and be friendly. More basics of friendship.

Or should I talk about needing to love yourself as you put yourself out there? Or should I tell her to make kind friends, those who inspire you to feel good about yourself, not those who tear you down?

What was the nut that would fill her sad cheeks?

Then a flash burst from my teenage memory banks, and I turned to my bookshelf. Tucked there, worn and weathered, lay *On Friendship*, edited by Louise Bachelder. It was given to eighteen-year-old me by eighteen-year-old Julie. She was my best friend.

Inside, knit together, were individual threads of the friendship blanket, of what it means to be a friend and get one back.

I found faded blue stars next to my favorites. One said simply, "'Stay' is a charming word in a friend's vocabulary," a quote from writer Amos Bronson Alcott. I still repeat it today.

Another, from author Hugh Black: "The method for the culture of friendship finds its best and briefest summary in the Golden Rule." Timeless and comprehensible, like Emerson's words.

Then this, from poet Alexander MacLean:

"He who gets and never gives
Will lose the truest friend that lives;
He who gives and never gets
Will sour his friendships with regrets;
Giving and getting, thus alone
A friendship lives—or dies a-moan!"

As I gazed backward through all the friendships that have worked or haven't, I realized this was an important nut. Friendship isn't one of those things you can do alone. You both must want to be friends in equal measure.

So often I hear teenagers—all agers really—complain that friends are unreliable, unavailable, untrustworthy, uninterested. You can be a friend, perhaps, in all its open-hearted caring, but that doesn't necessarily mean you'll get a friend back. The other half of the equation may not fall into place just fine. Maybe Emerson would add, "If it doesn't work out, you may need to look elsewhere." Too many people are out there to settle for little.

For what it was worth, I eventually told my niece she needed to give and to get. Not tit-for-tat, but reasonably teen-for-teen, then adult-for-adult, as time goes on.

Knowing

Julie, meantime, didn't turn out to be a keeper. Maybe we stopped giving and getting, or maybe we stopped liking each other's clothes. I mean, really, we were only eighteen years old.

A great park job

On the worst of days, I can give myself quite a boost by parallel parking my Honda in a space meant for a Harley. The only way the car could fit any tighter is by compressing it in a trash compacter and reconstituting it in a flood. Or perhaps, like a helicopter, it could hover above the exact 15.1 feet of space needed to lower the red machine as if it were a precious lunar module.

My talent goes way back.

As a teenager, armed with my friends and a Friday night curfew, I'd jump into my father's baby blue Chevy and head to the bowling alley where we'd just so happen to meet the neighborhood boys who were looking for us as much as we were looking for them.

As they leered, I'd shun all the easy spaces and head for the tiniest slot of visible asphalt. When I slid into position, smooth and swift, they'd stare dumbfounded that a silly cheerleader had been able to inch herself into a spot as big as a megaphone with the light airiness of a couple of pom-poms.

I am woman, watch me park.

I can still today get that same kick by slipping my wheels into a tiny crevice built for a tricycle. It can turn a whole day around. When I bragged to a neighbor about a very tricky maneuver, he said this: "Whatever it takes to massage your ego, no matter how small and insignificant."

I beg to differ. Any single thing that makes you feel young and feisty in sixty seconds and, in my case, helps me accept all the other things I screw up as a mechanically challenged female—truth so rude it hurts—is like a facelift.

Beating guys at their car game may be my answer to plastic surgery.

For example, at twenty-one, my lovesick roommate hauled me to Montego Bay to meet her new island boyfriend. Dangling a set of keys, he led us to the car *I'd* rented. But when I went to drive it, eased into the seat and cozied down, he pushed me sideways and took the wheel because, "In Jamaica the men do the driving, and you'll never be able to park on these narrow streets anyway."

I can still remember the tone in my voice—like giving a bad dog a command it can't refuse without a whipping—and the submission in his eyes when I barked him and his hanger-on sidekick into the back seat. Then I made sure my friend's margarita tryst barely lasted the weekend.

Small and insignificant?

But my favorite memory occurred a few years later when Bruce, one of my cooler guy friends, told me to "get out, I'll do it" when we needed to fit my brown Datsun into a skintight city spot. Wanting to please him, I hesitated for a moment, knowing it's something guys need to prove. Should I tolerate that?

Then a second later, with a smirk on my lips, steel in my eyes, and my old *"watch me park"* mantra pounding in my head, I spun that machine into its ready-made cocoon, edged it like a switchblade retracting into its case, so not a ray of sun or a drop of rain could fit front or back. Then I slammed the door, walked ten paces, turned around, and glared at his hangdog face.

Small and insignificant? Then or now, only if the car doesn't fit.

Pulling an all-nighter

P roms of the past may cross your mind when you watch kids and grandkids, and neighbors and nieces, leave the house in shoes they'll shed seconds after walking into "Midnight in Paris" or "Hollywood Nights."

My junior prom theme was "Underwater Paradise." According to one hot list, that's been updated to the more modern "Enchantment Under the Sea."

As things change so they remain the same.

Well, I have a trick that can take you right back to when John or Jeff arrived at the front door to plant a lilac corsage on your wrist and whisk you away in his father's car, even if his father was driving.

Pull an all-nighter. First risky chance you get. Not because you must, for some nasty emergency reason, but because you want to.

My senior prom ended at an all-night diner in Northeast Philadelphia with stiff droopy hair and bleeding feet. It felt dangerous, scary, naughty—stolen hours usually spent in a twin bed in my parent's split level, a pile of textbooks on the floor, a princess telephone near my head.

I'm here to report you can do it all over again. Pulling

an all-nighter, as I did after a depressing milestone birthday, felt as racy as it did decades ago. Even if this time I feared my price would be a zombie soul.

It started after Ray threw me a dancing party; he consulted every family member to pull it off. When it was over, the two of us, along with my friend Peggy who had flown in from San Francisco, proceeded to a trendy hotel bar where we curled up on sofas and spoke boldly and truthful, like how we look better now than we did all those years ago. At least our hair isn't teased and topped with a bow.

At first the room was filled with other zombies; by five in the morning, they were gone. We felt younger than them, hipper, cooler. Imbued with a sense of immortality, we wandered to a well-known dive with the dregs of the drugged-out, half-dressed overnight crowd. There we ate the kind of breakfast that precedes cardiac arrest—cheese on eggs, potatoes, gobs of real butter dripping off limp slices of toast.

Gorged, we watched the day come up amid the quiet alleys, the echo of delivery men clanging steel doors, the distant sound of high heels, the fear of strangers who were lost in their own stupor, maybe just as afraid of us.

It was after seven when we got home. There was nothing to do but get the day going.

I'm no virgin to an overnighter. As a radio journalist, I once had the graveyard shift, watching darkness switch to morning light and fill me with a remembrance that somewhere normal people were getting up at a normal time and having a normal life. It would revitalize me. Yet at some point during the day, I'd crash hard.

This time I was so filled with giddiness for having done it, so plumb pleased with myself for still having it in me, I felt too powerful to sleep, a superhuman being charged with guts and home-fried potatoes.

After all the years trying to make the waking hours fun, exciting, meaningful, here were these wasted hours I had forgotten were so stimulating and steamy, filled with the intoxicating spirit of wild adventure.

I talked about that all-nighter for days, a badge of honor, proof the old girl still has it in her, even if I'd pay for it. And oh, pay for it I did.

But I didn't care one zombie bit.

For the first time in a long time—for a girl constantly chasing a good night's rest—fun was more fun than sleeping.

Good friends overstay

"Always leave them wanting more" is a quote commonly attributed to the great circus showman P. T. Barnum.

The trapeze artists may be swinging, the clowns may be juggling, the acrobats may be tumbling, but now it's time to let the bug-eyed audience go home, dreaming of the next time they'll see people jump through hoops.

Others say it was maybe the musician Bobby Womack who said it, or perhaps Walt Disney—more top entertainers.

Some have put their own spin on the idea. How often do we hear "Don't overstay your welcome?" Or as Ben Franklin said, "Guests, like fish, begin to smell after three days."

We get the idea. Since we were kids, we've learned it's good to know when to leave, so people will invite you again and not be afraid you'll arrive with trunks and furniture.

I'd like to put my own spin on the concept and repeat a favorite line from writer Amos Bronson Alcott: "'Stay' is a charming word in a friend's vocabulary."

Or maybe I'm just trying to cover my tracks.

Because recently, I overstayed. I went to a friend's house, planning a quick hello, and didn't leave. They had other guests so they were quite busy. They didn't need us there, Ray and me. But we, apparently, needed them. After a long drive to pick up something at Dale and Karen's house, and after sensing a fun atmosphere there, we stayed. Too long. Next thing you knew we were joining them for dinner.

How do you know when you overstay? One hint is that people stop feeding you. Whatever is on the table is gone. No more chips or grapes or cheese to take their place. Not even a begrudging cup of tea.

In this case, the fun group was making dinner. We were not invited. But there we were. The host indicated perhaps some faraway place like Tonga needed us, but the hostess began setting new plates at the table, squeezing us in. We became confused.

Me: Do we run, or do we sit?

Ray: We should go.

Me: Okay, you first.

Ray: You first.

We wanted to sit, that was the problem. Otherwise, that old advice would have kicked in. We would have left through giant hoops of fire.

Ta-dah!

But we didn't. Where were our manners?

As we perched between their twirling and juggling, the balancing and clowning—trying to find our exit but not wanting to—I remembered other friends and family that did not leave our house, either.

They stayed and stayed under our tent, admitting they were overstaying, but not finding the get-up-and-go to leave. They were sunk into our deep couches, pillows askew on the ground, socks off, drinking more wine, telling another story, laughing as we were nodding off.

In the moment, I wished they would leave. Sometimes I picked up the food—*no more cookies for you!*—but still they stayed. I cleared off plates. Crumpled napkins in the trash. Talked of an early morning the next day. They stayed.

And as time has gone on, unexpectedly, these have become fond moments: people having such a good time at our house that they stay.

As I leaned on the door jamb on this new occasion—*Are we leaving, are we staying?*—I remembered my own overstayers, how comfortable they looked and how special that was. Despite the proper manners they knew they should follow—ignore the sword swallowers, forget the tightrope walkers—they felt too entertained, too at ease, to go.

And when all was said and done, in retrospect, that made us feel pretty darn special.

I knew Dale and Karen would forgive us because they are generous people, but we sincerely apologized and said, "Sorry, we were having too much fun to leave."

Knowing

I have an inkling though, as time goes on, as they review that night in their memory banks, they'll recall it as a time when we made them feel loved, wanted, appreciated. Their brand of circus worked!

And oh, I should have added, "You're welcome!"

Girl hikes

"What are you, like a size five?" said a new acquaintance named Cindy acting helpful with her hiking boots in her hand. "Of course, they're way too big for you, but just look."

"What size are they?" I whispered, afraid of the number.

"They're a nine."

"Hand 'em over," I said. Her eyes widened.

Here I am talking about feet and shoes again. But a short person with big feet must do some explaining.

"I have this toe thing that makes me go up a size in hiking boots," I said to Cindy, "and this ankle thing that demands extra support. Then there's this arch thing and a heel thing."

She listened then nodded her head: "I've got this toe thing, too, and a bunion thing and this really sensitive skin thing, but these boots don't bother them at all." She took off her socks to show me. We stared at her bunions, she looked at my flat feet. I showed her my weird second toe, longer than the big one, and she showed me her weird big toe. She explained this style is great for people with weird things. They're all-leather, they have toe guards, they fit around the ankles like Spanx.

"Why don't you take them for a spin and see what you think," Cindy urged. I hardly knew her, but we'd already bonded over weird feet. Good enough for me.

I took out her insoles and put in my super-duper orthotics. Then I pulled on my blister-protecting, low-tech Wigwam wool socks—like teddy bears for my feet—as ancient as the baby shoes I still own to prove I once had small flappers. I don't tell Cindy I keep those shoes; some things are secret.

As she watched, I laced up, which takes three hours and fifteen minutes except longer if you use the special cinching technique that demands you take courses in sailing, technical climbing, and calf roping. But it was okay because we were talking the whole time about the importance of stiffness.

Girls.

Cindy watched me leaving, started to go back to her computer to finish a work project, then smiled at me like a mother waving goodbye to a child. She then dropped her eyes and smiled at the boots. She'd just told me she'd lost her own girl hiking buddy whose knee blew out. She looked at me and remembered.

With Cindy's shoes on my feet, I remembered too. Something was transformed. Suddenly, my thoughts strayed to favorite hikes in other places with girlfriends. Fun hikes, scary hikes, dumb hikes. I recalled a wilderness trip when I tramped with a plaster cast on a broken foot, wrapped up with a green trash bag and masking tape so it wouldn't get moldy, which it did anyway. I refused to be left out.

And I remembered another girl hike waiting out a storm, eating avocados and corn chips under a tree. And another deep in the Rockies, all five girls topless. *If guys can do it*, we figured, *why not us?* One friend even compared sizes, and we weren't talking about feet. I was relieved. Even then I feared someone would point down at my big ones, except I often squashed them in, wore a size too tight, trying to hide that part of my body.

As I climbed uphill on this new day, I got a glimpse of the borrowed boots handling the rocks and was shocked to see they weren't my old ones. My mind was somewhere else. I was back eating avocados in the rain, laughing doubled over, chatting about love and work and pain and joy, and gloriously crying and hugging topless, then taking one more step on my giant paws.

When the hike was over, I slipped off Cindy's shoes and gave them a good hard look. I hardly knew they were on, they fit so well. And for a while I hardly knew it was today, but yesterday, when I rarely worried about shoes or weather or weird things but just went out and had a ball.

Yes, I announced to no one, *I believe these boots will work.*

Bootylicious

Aunts are a mother, a sister, and a best friend all rolled into one. I'm not making this up. I'm reading a poem given to me by two nieces and a nephew. It's hanging on my wall because I take the job seriously, which means I invited one of these young people shopping at the busiest time of year. That would be my then twenty-five-year-old niece Barrie, who couldn't find a thing to wear.

Being an aunt was easy when the kids were little. Swimming, ice cream, movies, "Stay up as late as you want and don't tell your mother."

Mothers, *schmothers*, who needs them?

An aunt will give you cupcakes for breakfast.

But that was then, and this was now, when a good aunt would trudge from Nordstrom to Bloomingdale's, clear across a packed mall, starving and limping, to help a niece score one new thing. This niece, like most of my family, is petite, and the hunt was on for clothes that weren't too baggy, too long, too wide, too loud. It's a tall order for a short person.

"We are not the problem," she declared. The problem is designers who think clothes should be either cutout and skintight or big, boxy, and blousy. She didn't want to be exposed like a peeled banana or covered-up like a melon.

We made a pact we would not be allowed lunch, dinner, or rich red wine until she bought one new thing. We agreed underwear was not a thing; the item had to be visible from the outside.

Again, I realized I take my job seriously. Mothers, they can't avoid. Grandmothers are visited, even if out of guilt. But aunts must strike out on their own and promise a different, wiser woman to rely on. In this case it meant shopping until my fingers ached from sliding hangers across sale racks. I had to secure one fabulous find that proved this aunt knows where to look.

"How about this?" I said, holding up a ruched gray knit dress I thought was super cute. "Too much fabric, too dull, too tight," she replied. We trudged on.

We went to Neiman Marcus for a laugh at the price tags. We found a dickie. My niece didn't know what a dickie was. I explained it's an odd neck covering big in the Sixties that slips inside a shirt in place of an underlayer. The Beatles used to wear them, I added. It's an easy solution for a dressed-up look. How wise am I!

And of course we found black, lots and lots of black, which we were sick of. We were searching for the un-black along with the un-dickie.

Some years ago, in another store in another place, a young woman marched up to me and said, "Are you my aunt?" Taken aback, I gently said "No." She thought I was a long-lost relative, perhaps one who would fill a void, even impart knowledge in an innocuous way not as annoying as her mother.

Hopeful and helpful, hip yet classy, an aunt tries to pull off a delicate balancing act.

Finally, my lovely niece tried on "dressy" jeans, the trickiest item in a girl's wardrobe. They must fit absolutely perfectly, cuddle every curve yet cover every pouch. She pranced up and down, glanced backward in every mirror, and I could have kissed those designer denims that hugged her in all the right round places.

We were jubilant, literally dancing in the aisles. And I thought being a good aunt could be as easy as an old-fashioned dickie, and as foolproof as the color black.

An aunt, I realized, must tell the truth about how bootylicious a butt looks in a pair of skintight dark blue jeans. And then if a winner is found—*thank the stars, whew!*—she must open her wallet and buy them.

The definition of joy

My oldest friend Elayne, my so-called "positive partner," and I continue to hope. We're determined to
look at the bright side of things, even if we need
to make ourselves miserable to do it. One of our projects
toward that end is "joy journals," the kind of thing you did
when you were thirteen years old, which is when we met,
and the kind of thing you forget about after thirteen when
you have joy nailed down. Which we don't.

So we continue to work on a grown-up definition of
this easy-to-toss around word that means different things
to different people and different things in different cultures,
perhaps, and different things one day to the next and different things even minute to minute. I've been so curious about
the proper way to explain this fleeting yet enviable goal, this
ephemeral thing, I've found myself in a state of constant
expectation, waiting for joy to bump me in the night.

Am I feeling joy now? Is this it? Am I doing it right?

When I was a little girl, my mother would cut a thick
wheel of ripe pineapple, wrap it in a napkin, and sit me
on the front stoop to watch the world go by. I still eat

pineapple that way today and get the same burst of—
what?—peace, glee, absorption?

I eat a slice and think, *Is this joy?*

Or maybe joy is the sense of wonder when I step outside
the back door and spy a hawk soaring on the wind, and my
breath stops. *Is that joy?* Does joy make you kick up your
heels, or is it satisfaction in the everyday?

And whatever it is, how in the world do we get more
of it?

Lots of questions, fewer answers.

As Elayne and I pushed closer to the truth, we looked up
the official definition of joy while chatting over FaceTime.
We were not sitting in her bedroom cleaning her closets like
we did decades ago. Disappointing. Instead, we opened a
few books, put our virtual heads together, and decided on
"extreme happiness." Then we realized we wanted it with
extreme greediness. The journals began. The idea was to
identify joy, own it, expand it.

The next day, I sat in my car in a crowded parking lot,
ready to begin a hike. The temperature was crisp yet warm,
lovely. But I was inside my hot car wondering how to get
what might be waiting on the other side of the window. *Was
joy out there?* I stayed in the car and pondered. The humor
didn't escape me. I laughed. *Was that joy?*

In yoga philosophy, the word for joy is contentment or
santosha, something I once thought was an excuse for not
getting what we truly want. Maybe it's still true. *Santosha*
is the ability to stay centered even if the pineapple isn't

sweet, if the swooping eagle is a crow eating the trash. It's not about achieving or acquiring. Most say it's about living in the present moment, without fear of the future or regret for the past.

Those moments, so rare, are said to last a lifetime, while the others quickly fade and disappear.

Later that day, I took out *The Book of Positive Quotations,* compiled by John Cook, and found a full forty pages on happiness, more than on hope, courage, success, every other topic. The adult search for happiness beats all.

I found this one: "Joy is the feeling of grinning on the inside," from author Melba Colgrove. And this from journalist Holbrook Jackson: "Those who seek happiness miss it, and those who discuss it, lack it." *Caught!* And this simple one from the ancient philosopher Seneca: "Learn how to feel joy."

I picked up my journal to see what I'd written so far, getting ready to share with Elayne:

- Swimming alone in a pool
- Hiking in the mountains
- Helping a friend find peace at a tough time
- Watching a tiny bird flutter on a tree limb
- Getting into bed early to read
- Having time and space without commitments

I closed the journal, realizing I'd loved these things forever.

Knowing

Outside, the sun was shining. I sliced a thick wheel of pineapple like Mom used to do for me, wrapped it in a napkin, and went out to watch the world go by. It made me feel good, that was all I knew for sure.

So much for growing up ...

David Bowie speaks

David Bowie said, "Aging is an extraordinary process whereby you become the person that you always should have been."

Since most of us spend our lives trying to actively, urgently become that person, I thought this disappointing. All the searching, all the striving for naught. Just think, the true you would have come along anyway, like a bus or a trolley, if only you'd waited long enough on the corner.

I thought about this as I chatted with a group of twenty-somethings at a party. Sweet, anxious, eager. Ready to become the people they were meant to be.

I didn't have the heart to tell them a big rock star said first they'd have to get old.

There was something so becoming about their becoming.

For example, they talked about what they want to do when they stop doing what they're doing now, about deciding what to give up and what to take on. They talked about where they want to live, what kind of person they want to love, looking for Mr. or Mrs. Right.

They talked about the freak show of speed dating and the hype of online dating. Of sitting at a bar for twenty minutes before realizing the person they were waiting for was sitting right there, looking nothing like their photo.

They talked about careers they hate and careers they would love instead. About working hard for something that mattered, or not working hard at all.

They talked about writing the great American novel instead of being a financial analyst. Of being a TV personality instead of a stockbroker, a musician instead of an accountant, a magician instead of a lawyer, a photographer instead of a teacher.

About having kids or not.

About wanting a life that's not boring, routine, poor, or suffocating.

About taking a break now that the first career, or relationship, or plan had failed. About following the next big idea full steam ahead as soon as they figure out what that is.

About finding time for passions. About doing what they want and not what they should do, or doing what they should do for now, so they have enough money to do what they want later. When they decide what that is.

About getting married soon or not at all. About being their own person, on their own terms, without compromise.

I wanted to tell them to be patient, that Bowie said it would all be revealed as they aged. The bus or trolley would come down the street and they'd get on.

But I also wanted to tell them what to do in between. Wait for the bus or pace back and forth? Stand on another street?

What's more fascinating than the subject of becoming ourselves? We're obsessed with it. Yet listening to all the angst and dreams, hopes and conundrums, I wondered why we can't find a shortcut so we don't have to wait years for answers. Why should we become just as we're ready to succumb? That doesn't sound fair, does it?

Can't we just download an app? Like, today?

I thought of Bowie's untimely departure and remembered he was an icon of individuality, of being himself. Maybe he had something more to say on the subject that could help me sound wise at that moment. I snuck in a corner with my phone and found this: "Make the best of every moment. We're not evolving. We're not going anywhere."

I didn't say it that way though, knowing no one would really listen—even if it was Bowie—or understand what it meant. Hell, I wasn't sure what it meant either.

Instead, I said the only thing I could think of that would become their becoming: *"Go for it!"*

Mom guilts us

How do you celebrate Mother's Day when the guest of honor is conspicuously absent? What if she's been gone from the scene or the seen for a full thirty years?

What exactly is the right way to get your arms around such a mom?

That was the question my sisters and I posed as we marked both Mother's Day and the thirtieth anniversary of Blanche's transition from a pixie in jeans and thick gray hair to the woman who appears in our dreams.

That's a long time, no see. A long time to be absolutely, completely, undeniably absent.

But was she?

"Mom, are you there?" teased my sister Shara. "Come on, Mom, give us a sign. You can do it."

As we leafed through her papers while huddled in my living room in the rain, surrounded by a ring of candles, wrapped in blankets, and sipping hot tea—this was what we wanted to know.

Was she watching over us while we were wondering about her?

We listened for something, anything. Nothing.

We proceeded with the next best thing, scanning through her photos on a day devoted to the one responsible for the three of us: Caryl the oldest, Shara the youngest, me sandwiched in the middle.

We were having a "Momfest."

There she was. Mom eating cantaloupe in a pink bathrobe, her cheeks as ripe as the fruit. Mom in a pale blue bathing suit, winking. Mom in a purple striped blouse, hugging Shara and me on either side, an arm around each of us. Mom, Dad, Caryl, and me at the New Jersey shore, acting silly. Mom skinny, Mom chubby, Mom as a baby, Mom first married, Mom right before she died of heart disease at fifty-seven.

"Look how cute you still were," exclaimed Caryl, to the mom who wasn't there.

We recalled Mom darning socks by the TV, Mom making steak sandwiches heavy with fried onions, Mom drawing paper dolls that had strangely square hands and feet, Mom refinishing old wood furniture, way before the distressed look was in.

We were sitting around the big coffee table Mom sanded and stained decades ago.

"Mom?" I said, peering upward. "Remember the time I was sick and far away and you, above anyone else, figured out what was wrong way before the Internet could make it easy?"

"And remember, Mom, the time I surprised you, knocking on your door when you hadn't seen me for a year? You acted like you'd won the lottery. I felt sainted, immortal."

"And remember, Mom, how you pulled the hair back off my face because you wanted to see as much of me as you possibly could?"

"Can you hear me, Mom?" I implored. We opened our eyes and ears for a sign.

The flicker of a candle, a clap of thunder, a bird singing, a dog's bark, a plate falling off the table.

The heater revved up. "That's it," screamed Shara. "Mom's starting the heater."

We would take anything.

We opened her handwritten will after so many years and skimmed the details—who gets the painting of the half-naked *senorita*, now staring from my wall; how each of us would inherit one of her three self-portraits in plaster, an uncanny likeness; where the bank accounts were; how she wanted to be cremated.

"Come on, Mom," Caryl pleaded. "You can do it."

She had given us signs before. Like after she died, when a cat showed up at our *shiva* house, a cat no one had seen before or after. Like when a bird, we swore, materialized from the ashes we tossed over the Schuylkill River near where she was born. Both were gray, like they were adorned with Mom hair.

We read again, for the first time in three decades, these words in her flowing hand: "I have to leave you with one last bit of guilt ..."

She went on: "My most important and final wish and hope is that the three of you continue to maintain contact and concern for each other, no matter how many miles or lifestyles may separate you. If you don't keep a sense of family among you then most of my time on earth will have been wasted."

"See you *are* here," I teased, knowing moms everywhere give their kids this guilt, but not every mom gets her wish.

We looked at each other. We couldn't deny that parts of Mom—no flicker, no thunder—were perched at her coffee table, staring at her self-portrait, sitting right there.

The three of us were together. We were the sign.

The meaning of life

You are insignificant, unnecessary, meaningless, and worse, temporary. Countless species are anxiously waiting for your obsolete kind to suddenly, mysteriously, eternally vanish—leaving but a few hieroglyphics, a handful of credit card bills, and a half-eaten container of gelato.

That's the message you get during a trip to the Smithsonian's National Museum of Natural History in Washington, D.C. It leads to huge questions, like why humans are the only species that need clothes. Every other creature is wash-and-wear. Some even get new customized coats every year, a perfect fit. You can't get that at Macy's no matter how good you are at higher math.

At the museum, you remember the dinosaurs were here for 150 million years and they were big, really big. Sharks, meantime, have been here 400 million years and they're big, too. We're here only 200 thousand years, and we're small, really small. If size matters, the only hope we have is the cockroach, 300 million years old. I never thought I'd envy roaches, but learning their skills could score a timeless position inside the bowels of a restaurant.

When you're done with the past, you head across the National Mall to the National Air and Space Museum to learn about the most beguiling subject in the universe: dark matter. That stuff that clearly is stuff but no one knows what kind of stuff only that surely it is stuff, so we give it an important scientific name: matter. And since stuff sounds sort of stuffy, we add an interesting adjective: dark. This explains everything.

I peered into the dome of the planetarium and wondered about the vastness of the universe. I was dizzy about whether we were going forward or backward as the stars exploded and the matter spread. I guess it all depended on whether the sharks were eating the roaches, or it was the other way around.

The reason we don't know what the matter is with the matter is that it's secretive. I wanted to reach up and say, "Matter matters! Take a chance, open up, be more vulnerable." The problem could be dark energy. That's what moves the matter around whether it wants to move or not. Again, this explains everything.

Once you're done exploring the past and the future, you walk outside on the National Mall and gaze at the U.S. Capital, standing big yet somehow small in the present moment.

If most of the species that ever did exist are long gone, and most of the species that ever will exist are unborn, it's hard to get excited about what's happening right now: politics, government, hazelnut gelato.

Knowing

The question of the curious meaning of life looms.

Fortunately, it's all been explained.

The author C.S. Lewis said, "If the whole universe has no meaning, we should never have found out that it has no meaning: just as, if there were no light in the universe and therefore no creatures with eyes, we should never know it was dark. Dark would be without meaning."

Again, this explains everything.

Whoa ... what?

In other words, if the sharks and cockroaches are ruling the past and probably the future, and Congress is ruling the present now that the dinosaurs are gone, there must be some light in the universe to solve all that's wrong in the dark world today.

Got it?

After You Read:
Rinse

D id you read? Some of it at least? It's important, because the amount you've allowed to seep in may have something to do with the amount of internal maintenance you need to do in the form of a brain rinse.

But what if you can't stand on your head to get that quick upside-down cleanse? Or have no intention of ever standing on your head? Maybe you can barely stand on your own three feet some days, and that's way enough of a challenge for many of us.

And yet, no matter how you do it, it is helpful to get a bat's eye view of the world now and again, when no other reasonable way of putting your mind on straight seems to work.

But how?

Go grab two thick blocks and let's try something. No blocks? How about two copies of *War and Peace* or an equally mammoth novel? Or if you gave those tomes away in high school, how about a chair? Yes, a chair seat will work just fine, so let's all start there.

Oh, and get a folded blanket.

Now put the blanket on the seat and take the chair near a wall. Stand with your back to the wall and place the chair seat in front of you. Make your feet wide, lean your butt against the wall, and extend your upper body toward the chair. Then cross your arms on the seat and rest the crown of your head on the blanket. Stay a while.

This pose is a mini standing forward bend with the head upside down, and it's called supported *uttanasana*.

Now, just stay ... one minute, two, five minutes is even better if nothing hurts. If your head doesn't reach the chair, go fatten up the support, perhaps add *Gone with the Wind* or some fluffy plush towels.

It feels like this: *Ahhh* ...

This may not be the exact scientific explanation, but I'd venture that when you stand back up, you'll feel someone has gotten in your head with a tiny tool and slid the gunk off the wires. And secured a couple of loose screws while they were in there.

Even if you're not convinced your brain has been soaped, scrubbed, rinsed, dried, ironed out, and put safely back into its protective hard-shell case, you can be sure you've reversed the sagging jowls for a moment and perhaps stimulated a bit of collagen production in the face.

And many of us would give up more than our brains for that amount of adjustment alone.

About the Author

In 2008—determined to cleanse the chaos in her mind by laughing at it—Donna Debs began writing the humor column "Upside Down" for several Philadelphia-area newspapers, including the *Daily Local News* and *The Times Herald*. *Wash Your Brain* is her first story collection.

Donna is also a former news reporter and editor for Philadelphia's KYW Radio, and, for twenty-five years, she owned a writing/communications company, working with major corporate and nonprofit clients. If you peek into her window—but please don't!—you may find Donna upside down in a headstand or handstand, trying to wash her brain that way, too. Since the mid 1990s, she has doubled as an Iyengar yoga teacher with an active yoga studio.

Find her at www.donnadebswriting.com

About the Illustrator

At the tender age of three, Los Angeles-based cartoonist Mike Goldstein drew his first comic strip, "Willy the Worm." From then on, he was hooked on creating wild and whacky drawings. Mike specializes in humorous illustrations, caricatures, and graphic novels. He also teaches drawing workshops for both children and adults. Mike sees the humor in everything, especially the politically incorrect. It was suggested he tame his wildest instincts for the illustrations in this book but hopes you won't think he's suddenly straightened up.

Find him at www.mjgillustration.com